Better Homes and Gardens®

Meals in Minutes

Treat guests to a dinner featuring *Shrimp-Filled Tortillas* (see recipe on page 63). Roll up shrimp filling inside tortillas, then deep-fat fry the tortillas and top with an avocado mixture.

On the cover: This fast and elegant dinner features *Easy Chicken Divan, Cran-Citrus Salad* served with honey-mayonnaise dressing, and purchased hard rolls. (See recipes on page 27.)

BETTER HOMES AND GARDENS BOOKS

Editorial Director: Don Dooley
Managing Editor: Malcolm E. Robinson   Art Director: John Berg
Asst. Managing Editor: Lawrence D. Clayton   Asst. Art Director: Randall Yontz
Food Editor: Nancy Morton
Senior Food Editor: Joyce Trollope
Associate Editors: Sharyl Heiken, Rosalie Riglin, Rosemary Corsiglia
Assistant Editors: Elizabeth Strait, Sandra Mapes
Designers: Harijs Priekulis, Tonya Rodriguez

CONTENTS

One Moment Please...

You get home late and the family's starved, unexpected guests arrive at mealtime, or you have to squeeze dinner in between the office and the club meeting—situations like these mean that you need to cook a tasty meal in a hurry. It's time someone helped you.

Help is here. Better Homes and Gardens has developed *Meals in Minutes*—for those of you who don't have much time to spend in the kitchen and for those who want to spend as little time cooking as possible.

As you look through this book, you'll see that the emphasis is on saving you time. Notice the Making Minutes Count ideas on pages 6 and 7. These ideas will help you trim precious minutes from meal preparation.

And note that there are 28 menus—breakfasts, brunches, luncheons, dinners, and suppers—each of which takes only 30 minutes to prepare. That's 30 minutes from when you walk into the kitchen until the complete meal is ready to put into serving dishes.

When you want to select a quick main dish and build your meal around it, turn to the Fast Main Dishes section. There, you will find a wide variety of flavorful main dishes. If you need a main dish to fit a particular time schedule, check page 92 for the preparation time of every main dish in the book.

Complete your meal by referring to the Rounding Out the Meal section. This recipe section contains quick-to-prepare salads, vegetables, breads, and desserts.

So, anytime you're short on meal preparation time, remember *Meals in Minutes*. It's here to help you.

A main dish made from planned overs

← Next time you prepare meat loaf, make extra so you'll have enough left for *Meat Loaf-Stuffed Tomatoes* (see recipe on page 76). Combine the cooked meat loaf with kidney beans, chili sauce, and chili powder, then fill the tomato shells.

Making Minutes Count

Remember, foods bake faster in smaller portions. You can cut time by baking meat loaf in muffin pans, desserts such as custard in small cups, and casseroles in individual baking dishes.

- Serve one-dish meals such as meat and vegetable combinations frequently. They save cooking, serving, and clean up time.
- Streamline meals by serving simple, yet hearty two-course menus. For example, serve a meat and vegetable main dish with a salad or a dessert. (Remember that fruit salads can double as desserts.)
- Serve things in big pieces when possible. For example, serve a melon wedge instead of a fruit cup for dessert and a wedge or a slice of lettuce instead of a mixture of torn greens for a salad.
- Freeze hamburger patties already shaped. Wrap each patty in clear plastic wrap or waxed paper. Then, pack the patties into a round container or plastic bag and seal.
- Wash lettuce and remove the core before refrigerating it in a plastic container.
- Use canned whole or boned chicken when recipes call for cooked chicken. The whole chicken will give prettier slices or cubes.

- Spending a little time each week planning and organizing your meals will save you a great deal of time in the long run. Sit down with a note pad, pencil, cook books, and grocery ads from the newspaper. Then, write down the menus and the shopping list for the week. This way you can do the week's shopping all at once, You'll know ahead of time what you're going to prepare for each meal, and you'll be sure to have everything on hand.
- Keep an orderly and efficient kitchen. Have duplicates of frequently used utensils such as dry and liquid measuring cups, spatulas, paring knives, mixing spoons, mixing bowls, and measuring spoons. Throw out or store utensils and equipment that you hardly ever use. Save steps by keeping frequently used equipment as close as possible to the starting point of each job. For example, keep the coffeepot, coffee, and measuring spoon near the sink.

To separate frozen vegetables quickly, place them in a colander and pour boiling water over. You can then add the vegetables to casseroles or top-of-the-range dishes to finish cooking.

Use a pressure cooker to prepare many dishes speedily (see index for specific recipes). To cool the pressure cooker quickly, hold it under cold running water as illustrated.

- Hard-cook several eggs at a time and keep them refrigerated until needed.
- Save time by cooking packaged precooked rice instead of long grain rice.
- Chill desserts, salads, and beverages quickly in the freezer.
- Use frozen chopped onion or green pepper, instant minced onion or garlic, and onion or garlic powder instead of taking the time to chop or mince them fresh.
- When precooking vegetables in butter or cooking oil, use a saucepan big enough to serve as a mixing bowl.
- Take advantage of cook-at-the-table dishes such as those made in the chafing dish, fondue pot, or wok.
- Microwave ovens are great time-savers. Besides cooking foods quickly, they also speedily defrost or heat frozen foods. Follow the manufacturer's instructions for operation of the microwave oven.
- The blender can help you shave minutes from many food preparation steps. Use it to quickly chop vegetables, crush crackers or make bread crumbs, combine ingredients for salad dressings, blend beverages, and perform many other tasks.

- Use trays to cut down on the number of trips from kitchen to table. For instance assemble the salad greens, dressing, salt, and pepper on a tray in the kitchen and then carry it to the table.
- Make easy sauces from canned soups. For example, serve cream of mushroom soup or cheese soup over cooked vegetables.
- Use a quarter-pound stick of butter or margarine when the recipe calls for ½ cup.
- Sprinkle dry mushroom, onion, or brown gravy mix into stews or hearty soups to both thicken and add flavor.
- Prepare barbecue sauce mix, then add horseradish for an extraordinary and easy seafood cocktail sauce.
- Dress up cooked potatoes by stirring in onion salad dressing and snipped parsley.
- Use blue cheese salad dressing as a topping for hamburgers or baked potatoes.
- For garlic bread, spread the bread with garlic-flavored salad dressing.
- Toss cooked vegetables with creamy French or cheese flavored salad dressing.
- Mix equal amounts of whipped cream and sweet French dressing for a luscious topping for fruit salads.

Whenever possible, avoid using extra dishes. For example, mix the milk, egg, and oil for muffins in the cup you measure the milk in, or carefully mix a casserole in the baking dish.

What do you think of when you're in a hurry at mealtime? Frozen dinners? Packaged main dishes? Carry-out foods? Next time, think home-cooking. By looking through this section, you'll see that you can indeed prepare a fast home-cooked meal. In fact, you can have any one of the 28 breakfast, brunch, luncheon, dinner, and supper menus ready to eat in only 30 minutes.

Sound hard? It's not. To ensure that everything's done on time, follow the preparation timetable under each menu. It shows the most efficient way to organize your time.

And, since quick meals and entertaining seldom seem to go together, you'll welcome the menus for speedy company meals that are in this section. These special menus are marked with the entertaining symbol.

30-Minute Meals

For a fast supper choose tasty Pizza Supper (see page 40). Delicious *Pizza-Rama* starts with frozen pizza, and *Creamy Dressing* is a bottled dressing fix-up.

Breakfasts and Brunches

SUNDAY BREAKFAST

Aebleskiver
Applesauce
Panfried Canadian-Style Bacon
Breakfast Mocha
or
Mock Orange Tea

PREPARATION TIMETABLE

Start timing: Assemble ingredients

At 5 minutes: Combine ingredients for
Breakfast Mocha or
Mock Orange Tea

At 10 minutes: Prepare Aebleskiver

At 20 minutes: Heat Breakfast Mocha or
Mock Orange Tea
Panfry bacon

At 30 minutes: Meal is ready to serve

Your family or guests are sure to enjoy this tasty breakfast featuring Danish doughnuts, called Aebleskiver, and a hot beverage.

Breakfast Mocha

1⅔ cups nonfat dry milk powder
⅓ cup unsweetened cocoa powder
⅓ cup sugar
2 to 3 teaspoons instant coffee
powder
2½ cups boiling water
Vanilla ice cream

Mix the first 4 ingredients; gradually stir in water. Heat through. Float small scoopful ice cream atop each serving. Serves 4.

Mock Orange Tea

4 teaspoons instant tea powder
2 teaspoons orange-flavored
breakfast drink powder
⅛ teaspoon ground cinnamon
Dash ground cloves
4 cups water
2 tablespoons honey

Mix first 4 ingredients; stir in water and honey. Heat through. Makes 4 servings.

Aebleskiver

⅔ cup packaged biscuit mix
¼ cup milk
2 egg yolks
2 tablespoons sugar
⅛ teaspoon ground cardamom
2 stiffly beaten egg whites
Butter or margarine
Powdered sugar

In mixer bowl combine first 5 ingredients; beat at low speed with electric mixer till mixed. Fold in egg whites. Grease cups in aebleskiver pan* with butter or margarine. Heat pan over medium heat. Fill cups ⅔ full of batter. Cook till bubbly, 2 to 3 minutes. Gently turn with 2 wooden picks. Cook till done, about 2 minutes more. Sprinkle with powdered sugar. Grease cups and repeat with remaining batter. Makes 12 to 14 aebleskiver (4 servings).

*Or, cook batter on greased griddle, using 2 tablespoons batter per pancake.

Danish breakfast delicacy

Mouth-watering *Aebleskiver* (Danish doughnuts) get their shape from the pan in which they are cooked. Dust the warm doughnuts with powdered sugar after removing them from pan.

SATURDAY BRUNCH

Triple Fruit Drink
or
Sherry Flip
or
Orange-Apricot Nog
Chicken Scramble
Melba Toast
Beverage

PREPARATION TIMETABLE

Start timing: Assemble ingredients

At 5 minutes: Make Orange-Apricot Nog
or Triple Fruit Drink
or Sherry Flip; re-
frigerate till served

At 8 minutes: Make Chicken Scramble

At 23 minutes: Cook Chicken Scramble

At 30 minutes: Meal is ready to serve

Take it easy some Saturday morning after a long week of getting the children to school or Dad to work, and combine breakfast and lunch with this brunch idea.

First, prepare your pick of the three beverage starter suggestions. Then, make the tasty Chicken Scramble with its colorful bits of green pepper and toasted almonds. All that's left to do is open the box of melba toast and pour the beverage.

Triple Fruit Drink

1 12-ounce can apricot nectar,
chilled (1½ cups)
1½ cups orange juice, chilled
2 tablespoons lemon juice

In a pitcher combine apricot nectar, orange juice, and lemon juice. Chill till served. Makes 6 servings.

Sherry Flip

1 6-ounce can frozen lemonade
concentrate
1 cup dry sherry
Ice cubes

Stir lemonade concentrate and sherry together till lemonade is melted. Serve mixture over ice cubes. Makes 6 servings.

Orange-Apricot Nog

1 orange, peeled and cut into small
pieces
1 16-ounce can apricot halves,
chilled
1 egg
½ cup cold milk
1 teaspoon vanilla

In blender container place orange and undrained apricots; blend till smooth. Add egg, milk, and vanilla. Blend 1 minute. Keep chilled till served. (Don't mix more than ½ hour before serving.) Serves 6.

Chicken Scramble

½ cup fresh or frozen chopped onion
½ cup fresh or frozen chopped green
pepper
⅓ cup slivered almonds
¼ cup butter or margarine
2½ cups cubed cooked chicken
¾ teaspoon salt
Dash pepper
• • •
6 slightly beaten eggs
½ cup grated Parmesan cheese

In medium skillet cook onion, green pepper, and almonds in butter till vegetables are tender but not brown. Add chicken, salt, and pepper; mix well. Cover and cook till chicken is heated through, 2 to 3 minutes. Meanwhile, combine eggs with Parmesan cheese; pour over chicken. Cook and stir gently over low heat till done, 7 to 10 minutes. Makes 6 servings.

SUMMER BRUNCH

Breakfast Fruit Cup
or
Melon Cup
Hominy-Cheese Special
Herbed Tomatoes
Beverage

PREPARATION TIMETABLE

Start timing: Preheat broiler
Assemble ingredients

At 5 minutes: Prepare Breakfast Fruit
Cup or Melon Cup; re-
frigerate till served

At 15 minutes: Prepare Herbed Tomatoes

At 20 minutes: Broil tomatoes
Prepare Hominy-Cheese
Special

At 30 minutes: Meal is ready to serve

Try this hurry-up brunch on one of those summer days when you want to spend as much time as possible outside. For the first course, prepare either a melon fruit cup splashed with orange-flavored liqueur or a combination fruit cup drizzled with a creamy yogurt topper. Then serve the broiled tomatoes topped with the special hominy-cheese sauce.

Melon Cup

2 cups cubed chilled cantaloupe
2 cups cubed chilled honeydew or
casaba melon
¼ cup orange-flavored liqueur

Combine the cantaloupe and honeydew or casaba cubes; pour orange-flavored liqueur over and chill till served. At serving time, spoon into dishes. Makes 4 servings.

Breakfast Fruit Cup

1 16-ounce can grapefruit sections,
chilled and drained
1 11-ounce can mandarin oranges,
chilled and drained
4 maraschino cherries, halved
• • •
½ cup pineapple-flavored yogurt
2 teaspoons sugar
2 teaspoons lemon juice
¼ cup shredded coconut

Combine first 3 ingredients; spoon into 4 sherbet dishes. Thoroughly mix the yogurt, sugar, and lemon juice. Spoon over fruit. Top with coconut. Makes 4 servings.

Hominy-Cheese Special

Drizzle this golden mixture over lightly browned Herbed Tomatoes—

1 10¾-ounce can condensed Cheddar
cheese soup
⅓ cup milk
1 16-ounce can hominy, drained
1 tablespoon instant minced onion

In medium saucepan combine soup and milk. Stir in hominy and onion. Cook, stirring occasionally, over medium heat till heated through and bubbly. Serve over Herbed Tomatoes. Makes 4 servings.

Herbed Tomatoes

Good with or without the hominy and cheese—

4 medium tomatoes
Salt
Pepper
1 tablespoon prepared mustard
2 tablespoons fine dry bread crumbs
½ teaspoon dried oregano, crushed

Preheat broiler. Halve tomatoes; place on baking sheet. Season with salt and pepper; spread with mustard. Mix crumbs and oregano; sprinkle over tomatoes. Broil 4 inches from heat till heated through and browned, about 10 minutes. Serves 4.

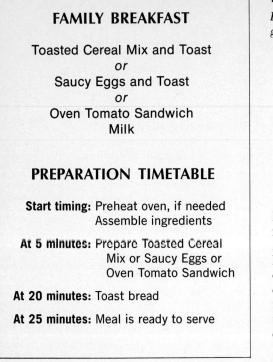

FAMILY BREAKFAST

Toasted Cereal Mix and Toast
or
Saucy Eggs and Toast
or
Oven Tomato Sandwich
Milk

PREPARATION TIMETABLE

Start timing: Preheat oven, if needed
Assemble ingredients

At 5 minutes: Prepare Toasted Cereal
Mix or Saucy Eggs or
Oven Tomato Sandwich

At 20 minutes: Toast bread

At 25 minutes: Meal is ready to serve

Looking for something unusual and delicious for that early-morning meal? Then, try the make-it-yourself cereal, poached eggs in mushroom sauce, or the sandwich from this breakfast menu. You are sure to like whichever dish you choose.

Toasted Cereal Mix

1½ cups quick-cooking rolled oats
½ cup chopped unroasted peanuts
½ cup chopped blanched almonds
½ cup wheat germ
½ cup raisins
⅓ cup snipped dried apricots
⅓ cup packed brown sugar
Light cream or milk

Preheat oven to 400°. Combine rolled oats, peanuts, almonds, and wheat germ. Spread in a 15½x10½x1-inch baking pan. Toast in a 400° oven for 10 minutes, stirring once. Stir in raisins, apricots, and brown sugar. Serve with light cream or milk. Serves 4.

Saucy Eggs

Poaching the eggs in a mushroom soup sauce gives them a delightful flavor—

1 10½-ounce can condensed cream of
mushroom soup
1 tablespoon instant minced onion
Dash pepper
½ cup milk
• • •
4 eggs
4 rusks
½ cup shredded natural Cheddar
cheese (2 ounces)

In medium skillet combine soup, instant minced onion, and pepper. Gradually add milk, blending well. Bring to boiling; reduce heat. One at a time, break eggs into small dish and gently slip into sauce. Cook, covered, over low heat till eggs are set, 10 to 12 minutes. To serve, place each egg on a rusk; top with sauce. Sprinkle with shredded cheese. Serves 4.

Oven Tomato Sandwich

Change the breakfast pace with a hot sandwich baked in the oven and topped with bacon—

8 slices bacon, cut in half
4 slices French bread, cut 1 inch
thick and buttered
4 thick slices tomato
• • •
½ cup mayonnaise or salad dressing
⅓ cup grated Parmesan cheese
2 tablespoons milk
1 tablespoon instant minced onion
1 teaspoon Worcestershire sauce

Preheat oven to 400°. Put separated bacon slices on a rack in shallow baking pan. Bake at 400° for 10 minutes. Meanwhile, put bread slices on baking sheet and toast on one side in oven, about 5 minutes. Remove bread from oven and turn; place tomato slices on untoasted sides. Combine mayonnaise, Parmesan, milk, onion, and Worcestershire. Spread over tomatoes. Bake sandwiches at 400° till golden, about 5 minutes. Top with bacon. Serves 4.

Nothing tastes better than hot soup on a cold winter day. So when the temperature drops, serve this brunch. Prepare either the ham and egg soup or the elegant pea and seafood soup. Complete the meal with English muffins and a cranberry spread.

Pea Soup Elegante

1 11¼-ounce can condensed green
  pea soup
1 10½-ounce can condensed cream of
  chicken soup
1 10½-ounce can condensed beef
  broth
2 cups light cream or milk
1 7½-ounce can crab meat, drained,
  flaked, and cartilage removed
¼ cup dry sherry
2 tablespoons butter or margarine

In saucepan combine green pea and cream of chicken soups; stir in beef broth and light cream. Cook and stir till heated through. Add crab, sherry, and butter or margarine; heat through. Makes 6 servings.

Cran Spread

¾ cup cranberry-orange relish
¼ cup soft-spread margarine
1 tablespoon sugar
¼ teaspoon ground cinnamon

In small bowl stir together cranberry-orange relish, soft-spread margarine, sugar, and cinnamon. Makes 1 cup.

Cream of Ham Soup

¼ cup butter or margarine
¼ cup all-purpose flour
1 teaspoon instant minced onion
5 cups milk
2 cups diced fully cooked ham
2 hard-cooked eggs, coarsely chopped
  Toasted round oat cereal

In saucepan melt butter. Blend in flour, onion, ½ teaspoon salt, and dash pepper. Add milk all at once. Cook and stir till thick and bubbly. Add ham and eggs; heat. Garnish with cereal. Serves 6.

Treat your family to hearty *Cream of Ham Soup* some winter morning. The toasted round oat cereal garnish adds a breakfast touch.

Luncheons

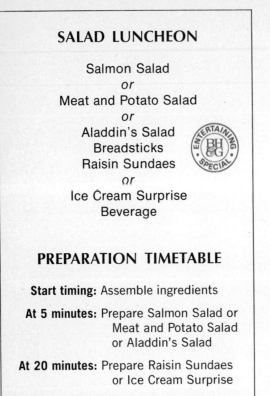

SALAD LUNCHEON

Salmon Salad
or
Meat and Potato Salad
or
Aladdin's Salad
Breadsticks
Raisin Sundaes
or
Ice Cream Surprise
Beverage

PREPARATION TIMETABLE

Start timing: Assemble ingredients

At 5 minutes: Prepare Salmon Salad or
Meat and Potato Salad
or Aladdin's Salad

At 20 minutes: Prepare Raisin Sundaes
or Ice Cream Surprise

At 30 minutes: Meal is ready to serve

Luncheon guests will be delighted when you serve them this tasty menu. Three main dish salads and two dessert recipes are offered. Prepare your choice.

Meat and Potato Salad

Combine two 16-ounce cans chilled German-style potato salad and one 12-ounce can chilled luncheon meat, cut in strips. On *each* of 6 individual plates, place 1 large tomato slice in a lettuce cup. Top with potato salad-meat mixture. Sprinkle salads with ½ cup shredded natural Cheddar cheese (2 ounces). Chill till served. Serves 6.

Aladdin's Salad
A tasty meat-cheese-lettuce salad —

1 small head lettuce, torn in bite-size pieces
4 ounces bologna, cut in strips
4 ounces sliced salami, cut in strips
1 4-ounce package shredded natural mozzarella cheese (1 cup)
2 hard-cooked eggs, sliced
Freshly ground pepper
⅓ cup mayonnaise or salad dressing
¼ cup creamy French salad dressing

Place lettuce in salad bowl. Atop lettuce group the bologna, salami, cheese, and egg slices. Season with pepper. Combine mayonnaise and creamy French salad dressing; spoon over salad and toss lightly. Chill till served. Makes 6 servings.

Salmon Salad
Water chestnuts and celery add crunch —

1 16-ounce can salmon, chilled and drained
2 7½-ounce cans minced clams, chilled and drained
1 8½-ounce can water chestnuts, drained and sliced
½ cup sliced celery
2 hard-cooked eggs, chopped
1 cup mayonnaise or salad dressing
1 tablespoon lemon juice
Lettuce
1 lemon, cut in wedges (optional)

Break salmon into chunks. In bowl combine salmon, clams, water chestnuts, celery, and eggs. Combine mayonnaise and lemon juice; add to salmon mixture, tossing lightly. Serve in individual lettuce-lined icers or bowls. Top with additional mayonnaise and pass lemon wedges, if desired. Chill till served. Serves 6.

Raisin Sundaes

½ cup light raisins
½ cup cold water
⅓ cup rum
¼ cup packed brown sugar
1 tablespoon cornstarch
2 tablespoons butter or margarine
Vanilla ice cream

Soak raisins in mixture of water and rum till plump, about 5 minutes. Mix brown sugar and cornstarch; add to raisin-rum mixture. Cook and stir till bubbly. Add butter. To serve, spoon over ice cream. Serves 6.

Ice Cream Surprise

Prepared in the blender in just minutes —

2 jiggers brandy (3 ounces)
2 jiggers crème de cacao (3 ounces)
1 jigger orange-flavored liqueur
   (1½ ounces)
1 quart vanilla ice cream

Combine the brandy, crème de cacao, and orange-flavored liqueur in blender container; add vanilla ice cream, a scoop at a time, blending just till smooth. Serve at once in stemmed glasses or place in freezer till served. Makes 6 servings.

Keep *Salmon Salad* chilled in individual icers filled with crushed ice. The delectable mixture, nestled in a crisp lettuce leaf, contains salmon, clams, hard-cooked eggs, sliced celery, and water chestnuts.

SOUP-SANDWICH LUNCHEON

Crispy Grilled Ham and Cheese
Speedy Pea Soup
or
Cream of Pumpkin Soup
Beverage

PREPARATION TIMETABLE

Start timing: Assemble ingredients

At 5 minutes: Prepare Crispy Grilled
Ham and Cheese until
ready to dip in egg

At 15 minutes: Make Speedy Pea Soup or
Cream of Pumpkin Soup

At 20 minutes: Dip sandwiches in egg
and chips; grill

At 30 minutes: Meal is ready to serve

Soup and sandwiches are great favorites for luncheon, so try this menu. Prepare either the creamy pea soup topped with crunchy croutons or the unusual pumpkin soup topped with nutmeg. Serve the soup with the satisfying hot ham and cheese sandwich coated with potato chips.

Cream of Pumpkin Soup

1 13¾-ounce can chicken broth
   (1¾ cups)
1 16-ounce can pumpkin
1 cup milk
1 teaspoon salt
⅛ teaspoon pepper
   Ground nutmeg

In medium saucepan gradually stir chicken broth into pumpkin. Add milk, salt, and pepper. Bring to boiling over medium high heat, stirring occasionally. Serve in bowls; sprinkle with nutmeg. Makes 4 servings.

Speedy Pea Soup

Start with a can of peas and a blender to make this creamy pea soup—

1 17-ounce can peas
1 cup milk
½ small onion
2 tablespoons butter or margarine
½ teaspoon salt
   Dash garlic powder
   Dash pepper
       • • •
½ cup croutons

Combine peas, milk, onion, butter or margarine, salt, garlic powder, and pepper in blender container. Cover and blend till smooth, about 1 minute. Pour into 1½-quart saucepan. Heat through. To serve, pour hot mixture into soup bowls and top with croutons. Makes 4 servings.

Crispy Grilled Ham and Cheese

Perk up ham and cheese with mustard, tomato, and a crushed potato chip coating—

8 slices white bread
   Butter or margarine, softened
   Prepared mustard
4 thin slices boiled ham
4 slices process American cheese
   (4 ounces)
8 thin slices tomato
   Salt
       • • •
2 slightly beaten eggs
2 tablespoons milk
   Dash onion salt
2½ cups potato chips, crushed

Spread bread slices with butter. Then, spread 4 of the slices with prepared mustard; top *each of these* with 1 slice ham, 1 slice cheese, and 2 slices tomato. Sprinkle tomato with a little salt; top with second slice of bread. Combine slightly beaten eggs, milk, and onion salt. Dip both sides of sandwich in egg mixture, then in crushed potato chips. Grill on hot buttered griddle or skillet till golden brown on both sides, 3 to 4 minutes on each side. Makes 4 sandwiches.

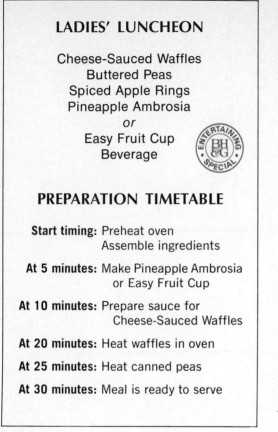

LADIES' LUNCHEON

Cheese-Sauced Waffles
Buttered Peas
Spiced Apple Rings
Pineapple Ambrosia
or
Easy Fruit Cup
Beverage

PREPARATION TIMETABLE

Start timing: Preheat oven
Assemble ingredients

At 5 minutes: Make Pineapple Ambrosia
or Easy Fruit Cup

At 10 minutes: Prepare sauce for
Cheese-Sauced Waffles

At 20 minutes: Heat waffles in oven

At 25 minutes: Heat canned peas

At 30 minutes: Meal is ready to serve

Treat your luncheon guests to this easy and elegant menu. Frozen waffles and Welsh rarebit give you a head start on the main dish, while canned and frozen fruits make up the luscious dessert.

Pineapple Ambrosia

1 20½-ounce can pineapple chunks
(juice pack), chilled
1 11-ounce can mandarin orange
sections, drained
2 bananas, sliced
¼ cup flaked coconut
3 tablespoons orange-flavored
liqueur

In bowl combine undrained pineapple, mandarin oranges, bananas, coconut, and liqueur. Toss lightly. Chill. Makes 6 servings.

Easy Fruit Cup

Bring out your prettiest glass bowl when you serve this refreshing fruit combination. Or, spoon the fruit into individual dishes—

1 30-ounce can peach slices, chilled
and drained
2 10-ounce packages frozen strawberries, partially thawed
• • •
1 7-ounce bottle lemon-lime
carbonated beverage, chilled
• • •
Sifted powdered sugar

In serving bowl combine peach slices and partially thawed strawberries; chill till served. Just before serving, pour chilled lemon-lime carbonated beverage over peach slices and strawberries in bowl. Sprinkle mixture lightly with sifted powdered sugar. Serve immediately. Makes 6 servings.

Cheese-Sauced Waffles

Stir shrimp, mushrooms, and chives into golden cheese rarebit before serving over hot-from-the-oven waffles—

12 frozen waffles
• • •
1 10-ounce package frozen Welsh
rarebit
• • •
2 4½-ounce cans shrimp, drained
1 3-ounce can sliced mushrooms,
drained
1 tablespoon freeze-dried chives

Prepare frozen waffles according to package directions for oven method. Meanwhile, cover bottom of large skillet with ¾ inch water. Loosen cardboard lid on frozen Welsh rarebit, but leave in place. Place frozen Welsh rarebit container in skillet. Cover skillet. Bring water to boiling. Boil rapidly for 10 minutes. Remove cardboard lid; pour rarebit into a saucepan.

Stir drained shrimp, sliced mushrooms, and freeze-dried chives into rarebit in saucepan. Heat through. Serve cheese-shrimp sauce over waffles. Makes 6 servings.

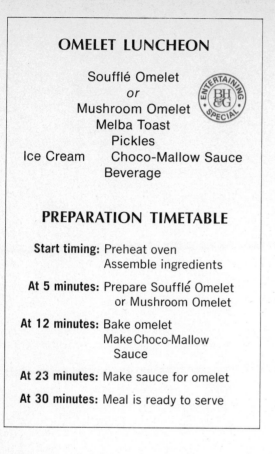

OMELET LUNCHEON

Soufflé Omelet
or
Mushroom Omelet
Melba Toast
Pickles
Ice Cream   Choco-Mallow Sauce
Beverage

PREPARATION TIMETABLE

Start timing: Preheat oven
Assemble ingredients

At 5 minutes: Prepare Soufflé Omelet
or Mushroom Omelet

At 12 minutes: Bake omelet
Make Choco-Mallow
Sauce

At 23 minutes: Make sauce for omelet

At 30 minutes: Meal is ready to serve

The most difficult part of preparing this menu is choosing between the egg-cheese omelet and the mushroom omelet.

Choco-Mallow Sauce

In saucepan combine one 7-, 9-, or 10-ounce jar marshmallow creme, ½ cup milk chocolate pieces, and 2 tablespoons milk. Stir over low heat till smooth. Remove from heat; stir in ¼ teaspoon vanilla. Serve over vanilla ice cream. Makes 1½ cups.

Tender baked egg dish

← Surprise family or guests with this puffy *Soufflé Omelet* served with a smooth cheese sauce. Baking the omelet in a round baking dish rather than a soufflé dish cuts time.

Mushroom Omelet

4 egg whites
4 slightly beaten egg yolks
2 10½-ounce cans condensed cream of
mushroom soup
• • •
½ cup dairy sour cream
1 5-ounce can boned chicken, drained
and cut into pieces

Preheat oven to 400°. Beat egg whites till stiff but not dry. Stir yolks into *1 cup* of the soup; then fold gently into egg whites. Turn into *ungreased* 9x1½-inch round baking dish. Bake at 400° till puffy and golden brown, 15 to 20 minutes. Meanwhile, in small saucepan mix remaining soup and sour cream; heat and stir till smooth. Add chicken; heat through. Serve over baked omelet. Makes 4 to 6 servings.

Soufflé Omelet

¼ cup butter or margarine
⅓ cup all-purpose flour
½ teaspoon salt
Dash pepper
2 cups milk
4 slightly beaten egg yolks
4 egg whites
1 cup shredded natural Cheddar
cheese (4 ounces)
⅓ to ½ cup milk

Preheat oven to 400°. Melt butter or margarine; blend in flour, salt, and pepper. Add the 2 cups milk all at once and cook, stirring constantly, till thickened and bubbly. Pour 1 cup sauce into small bowl; stir in yolks. (Set aside remaining sauce in saucepan.) Beat egg whites till stiff but not dry. Gently fold yolk mixture into beaten egg whites. Turn into *ungreased* 8x1½-inch round baking dish. Bake at 400° till puffy and golden brown, about 15 minutes.

Meanwhile, stir cheese into remaining sauce in pan; heat, stirring frequently, till melted. Thin to desired consistency with the ⅓ to ½ cup milk; heat. Serve over omelet. Makes 4 to 6 servings.

Need a quick luncheon for one of those rare days when the whole family's home? Try this one. Everyone is sure to enjoy it. The main dish is an open-face sandwich consisting of creamed tuna and mixed vegetables served over an English muffin. And the dessert features a sundae sauce with pears instead of ice cream.

Choco-Pear Sundaes

Reserved canned pear syrup is added to a fudge topping-honey-orange peel mixture to make a delectable sundae sauce—

1 16-ounce can pear halves, chilled
¼ cup fudge topping
2 tablespoons honey
½ teaspoon grated orange peel

Drain pears, reserving syrup. In small bowl combine fudge topping, honey, and orange peel. Add 1 to 2 teaspoons reserved pear syrup to thin. Just before serving, spoon topping over pear halves in dessert dishes. Makes 4 servings.

Polka-Dot Tuna
A fun to eat open-face sandwich—

1 8-ounce package frozen mixed
vegetables with onion sauce
1⅔ cups milk
1 tablespoon cornstarch
1 tablespoon cold water
• • •
1 6½- or 7-ounce can tuna, drained
and flaked
1 3-ounce can sliced mushrooms,
drained
2 tablespoons chopped canned
pimiento
• • •
4 English muffins, split, toasted,
and buttered
2 tablespoons toasted slivered
almonds (optional)

In saucepan combine frozen mixed vegetables in onion sauce and milk. Stir together cornstarch and water; add to vegetables. Cook and stir till thickened and bubbly.
Stir in tuna, sliced mushrooms, and chopped pimiento; heat through. Spoon over English muffin halves. Top with almonds, if desired. Makes 4 servings.

To add some crunch to *Polka-Dot Tuna,* sprinkle it with toasted almonds, and serve crisp celery and radishes as accompaniments.

```
┌─────────────────────────────────┐
│                                 │
│      SANDWICH LUNCHEON          │
│                                 │
│      Steak Dip Sandwiches       │
│       Corn-Aspic Salad          │
│              or                 │
│       Creamy Bean Salad         │
│           Beverage              │
│                                 │
│                                 │
│    PREPARATION TIMETABLE        │
│                                 │
│  Start timing: Preheat broiler  │
│                Assemble ingredients │
│                                 │
│  At 5 minutes: Make Corn-Aspic Salad │
│                or Creamy Bean Salad; │
│                chill till served│
│                                 │
│  At 10 minutes: Prepare Steak Dip Sand- │
│                 wiches—first toast │
│                 bread, then grill │
│                 steak and make sauce │
│                                 │
│  At 25 minutes: Meal is ready to serve │
│                                 │
└─────────────────────────────────┘
```

A busy morning's work calls for a hearty luncheon such as this satisfying salad and sandwich combination. Whether you've been raking leaves on a fall day or breaking spring ground for a garden, you need only excuse yourself from the work at hand for 25 minutes to prepare this meal.

Corn-Aspic Salad

Cut canned tomato aspic into cubes and toss with corn and salad dressing for this salad—

½ cup creamy French salad dressing
1 12-ounce can whole kernel corn, chilled and drained
1 12-ounce can tomato aspic, chilled
Lettuce

Pour French dressing over drained corn. Cut aspic into cubes. Toss lightly with corn mixture. To serve, heap salad in lettuce-lined salad bowl. Makes 6 servings.

Creamy Bean Salad

Toss two different kinds of canned beans together with a little chopped pimiento and then add creamy salad dressing—

1 16-ounce can lima beans, chilled and drained
1 16-ounce can French-style or cut green beans, chilled and drained
2 tablespoons chopped canned pimiento
• • •
⅓ cup creamy onion salad dressing

In large bowl combine lima beans, French-style or cut green beans, and chopped pimiento. Gently toss mixture with creamy onion salad dressing. Chill mixture till served. Makes 6 servings.

Steak Dip Sandwiches

Dip slices of toasted French bread into a sauce before topping them with sizzling steak pieces. Spoon additional sauce atop—

6 slices French bread, cut 1½ inches thick
Shortening
6 pieces beef sirloin steak, cut ¼ inch thick (about 1½ pounds)
• • •
½ cup butter or margarine
¼ cup water
3 tablespoons bottled steak sauce
2 tablespoons sliced green onion with tops
1 tablespoon Worcestershire sauce
¼ teaspoon salt

Preheat broiler. Toast French bread in broiler. Preheat griddle or electric skillet to 400°; grease lightly with shortening. Grill steak on griddle 2 to 3 minutes on each side.

In small saucepan combine butter or margarine, water, bottled steak sauce, sliced green onion with tops, Worcestershire sauce, and salt; heat through.

Dip toast slices in sauce; place on serving plate. Top *each* slice toast with grilled sirloin steak piece. Spoon remaining sauce atop steak. Makes 6 servings.

Dinners

Poached Fish
with
Almond Sauce   *or*   Wine Sauce
or
Herbed Tomato Sauce
Buttered Green Beans
Oven-Fried Frozen French Fries
Prune-Apricot Combo
or
Mocha Dessert
Beverage

PREPARATION TIMETABLE

Start timing: Preheat oven
Assemble ingredients

At 5 minutes: Make Mocha Dessert or
Prune-Apricot Combo

At 13 minutes: Heat frozen French
fries in oven

At 17 minutes: Poach fish

At 20 minutes: Prepare Almond Sauce or
Wine Sauce or Herbed
Tomato Sauce

At 25 minutes: Heat canned green beans

At 30 minutes: Meal is ready to serve

Want to prepare frozen fish in a different, easy-to-fix way? Then, serve Poached Fish. For just the right complement to the delicate flavor of the fish, prepare Almond Sauce, Wine Sauce, or Herbed Tomato Sauce. All three are delicious.

The main dish takes only 13 minutes to prepare, so you'll have plenty of time to fix the vegetable, potatoes, and dessert.

Poached Fish

Separate 4 frozen halibut steaks; put in skillet with just enough water to cover. Add ½ teaspoon salt. Bring to a boil; reduce heat. Cover; simmer till fish flakes easily when tested with fork, 7 to 8 minutes. Drain; serve with sauce. Serves 4.

Wine Sauce

Melt 1 tablespoon butter; blend in 1 tablespoon all-purpose flour. Add ½ cup milk and 2 tablespoons dry white wine; cook and stir till bubbly. Add ½ cup shredded process Swiss cheese (2 ounces); stir till melted. Serve over Poached Fish; sprinkle with paprika. Makes 1½ cups.

Prune-Apricot Combo

1 16-ounce jar stewed prunes
1 16-ounce can apricot halves
1 inch stick cinnamon
1 tablespoon lemon juice
2 tablespoons rum or brandy

Drain prunes and apricots, reserving ¼ *cup syrup from each*. Combine reserved syrups, cinnamon, and juice. Simmer 2 to 3 minutes. Remove from heat; add rum or brandy. Pour over fruits. Serve warm. Serves 4.

Mocha Dessert

1 17-ounce can chocolate pudding,
chilled
2 teaspoons instant coffee powder
1 cup frozen whipped topping, thawed
¼ cup chopped walnuts

Combine first 2 ingredients. Fold in topping and nuts. Spoon into sherbet glasses. Chill in freezer till served. Serves 4.

Dress up *Poached Fish* with delectable *Almond Sauce*. While the fish steaks are cooking, prepare the simple sauce quickly in the blender. Just before serving, sprinkle toasted sliced almonds atop the fish.

Herbed Tomato Sauce

    1 8-ounce can tomato sauce with
       chopped onion
    1 3-ounce can sliced mushrooms,
       drained
    ½ teaspoon sugar
    ¼ teaspoon salt
    ¼ teaspoon dried oregano, crushed
       Dash pepper
    ¼ cup shredded natural Cheddar
       cheese (1 ounce)

In saucepan combine tomato sauce with chopped onion, sliced mushrooms, sugar, salt, crushed oregano, and pepper; simmer 5 minutes. Spoon sauce over Poached Fish; sprinkle with shredded natural Cheddar cheese. Makes about 1 cup sauce.

Almond Sauce

    2 egg yolks
    1 tablespoon lemon juice
    ¼ teaspoon prepared mustard
       Dash cayenne
    6 tablespoons butter or margarine
    2 tablespoons sliced almonds,
       toasted

In blender container blend first 4 ingredients till mixed. Heat butter till almost boiling. With lid partly covering the opening and blender running slowly, pour ⅓ *of the hot butter*, in a thin stream, into blender container. Turn blender to high speed; slowly pour in remaining hot butter, blending till thick. Serve over Poached Fish. Top with nuts. Makes ⅔ cup.

ORIENTAL-STYLE DINNER

Chicken Livers Especial
or
Fragrant Beef
Buttered Rice
Deluxe Salad Toss
Spiced Crab Apples
Orange Sherbet   Fortune Cookies
Hot Tea

PREPARATION TIMETABLE

Start timing: Assemble ingredients

At 5 minutes: Make Deluxe Salad Toss;
chill till served

At 10 minutes: Put rice on to cook
Cut beef for Fragrant
Beef or chicken
livers for Chicken
Livers Especial

At 15 minutes: Finish making Fragrant
Beef or Chicken
Livers Especial

At 30 minutes: Meal is ready to serve

Long ago, the Orientals perfected a quick-cooking technique called stir-frying. Now, you can learn this technique by preparing Fragrant Beef or Chicken Livers Especial. For an unusual touch, cook the main dish in a wok at the table.

Deluxe Salad Toss

Pour boiling water over one 6-ounce package frozen pea pods; let stand 2 minutes, then drain well. Meanwhile, mix ¼ cup mayonnaise, ¼ cup dairy sour cream, and ½ teaspoon celery seed. Combine 3 cups torn lettuce, ⅓ cup sliced water chestnuts, and the pea pods. At serving time, toss with mayonnaise mixture. Serves 4.

Chicken Livers Especial

Serve this over the buttered rice —

½ cup fresh or frozen chopped green
pepper
⅛ teaspoon garlic powder
2 tablespoons cooking oil
1 pound chicken livers, halved
• • •
1 tablespoon instant minced onion
2 teaspoons cornstarch
½ teaspoon salt
Dash pepper
Dash curry powder
½ cup cold water
¼ cup dry white wine
1 teaspoon soy sauce

In a heavy skillet or wok cook chopped green pepper and garlic powder in hot oil about 2 minutes. Add halved chicken livers. Cook till green pepper is tender and chicken livers are lightly browned. *Do not overcook.* Combine instant minced onion, cornstarch, salt, pepper, and curry powder; stir in cold water, dry white wine, and soy sauce. Add this mixture to chicken liver mixture in the skillet. Cook and stir till the mixture thickens and bubbles. Serve immediately over hot rice. Makes 4 servings.

Fragrant Beef

For a special touch, cook this in a wok —

1 pound beef sirloin or round steak,
cut ½ inch thick
3 tablespoons soy sauce
3 tablespoons cold water
1 tablespoon cornstarch
½ teaspoon ground ginger
• • •
2 tablespoons cooking oil
2 tablespoons snipped green onion
tops

Slice beef into ¼-inch-wide strips. Blend soy sauce, water, cornstarch, and ginger; toss with beef to coat well. Heat oil in heavy skillet or wok. Add beef and stir-fry till brown, 5 to 6 minutes. Sprinkle with onion tops. Makes 4 servings.

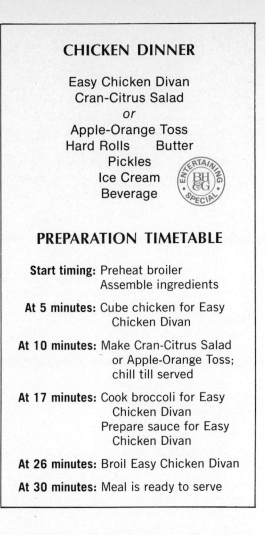

CHICKEN DINNER

Easy Chicken Divan
Cran-Citrus Salad
or
Apple-Orange Toss
Hard Rolls   Butter
Pickles
Ice Cream
Beverage

PREPARATION TIMETABLE

Start timing: Preheat broiler
Assemble ingredients

At 5 minutes: Cube chicken for Easy
Chicken Divan

At 10 minutes: Make Cran-Citrus Salad
or Apple-Orange Toss;
chill till served

At 17 minutes: Cook broccoli for Easy
Chicken Divan
Prepare sauce for Easy
Chicken Divan

At 26 minutes: Broil Easy Chicken Divan

At 30 minutes: Meal is ready to serve

Company coming and you need a special, quick-to-prepare meal? This menu is the answer to your problem. It's not only quick and delicious, it's also very attractive (see front cover photograph).

One of the main shortcuts of this elegant menu is that the Easy Chicken Divan combines the meat and vegetable into one dish. To make this dish pretty, use the meat from a canned whole chicken. The canned chicken is completely cooked, so it will take you just a few minutes to take the chicken off the bone and cube it.

To complete the menu, prepare one of the fruit salads given, and add purchased hard rolls, pickles, your favorite ice cream, and a hot or cold beverage.

Easy Chicken Divan

This attractive dish is shown on the cover—

2 10-ounce packages frozen broccoli
spears
2 packages hollandaise sauce mix
(*each* enough for 1 cup sauce)
1 cup dairy sour cream
½ cup dry sherry
¼ teaspoon ground nutmeg
3 cups cubed cooked chicken
½ cup grated Parmesan cheese
Butter or margarine

Preheat broiler. Cook broccoli according to package directions. Meanwhile, prepare hollandaise sauce mix according to package directions. Stir in sour cream, sherry, and nutmeg. Stir in chicken: heat through. Drain broccoli: arrange on ovenproof platter. Top with chicken-sauce mixture. Sprinkle with Parmesan: dot with butter. Broil 4 inches from heat till bubbly, about 3 minutes. Makes 6 servings.

Cran-Citrus Salad

This salad arrangement is shown on the cover—

1 16-ounce can orange and grapefruit
sections, chilled and drained
1 16-ounce can jellied cranberry sauce,
chilled and cut into 6 slices
Lettuce
½ cup mayonnaise or salad dressing
¼ cup honey
1 tablespoon vinegar

Arrange fruit and cranberry slices on lettuce-lined plate. Combine remaining ingredients; serve as dressing. Serves 6.

Apple-Orange Toss

Combine 2 large apples, cored and cut into bit-sized pieces; one 11-ounce can chilled mandarin orange sections, drained; and ¼ cup walnut pieces. Stir together ½ cup orange-flavored yogurt and 2 tablespoons orange marmalade; toss with apple-orange mixture. Makes 6 servings.

SUNDAY DINNER

Ham in Stuffing Shells
Buttered Beets
Lettuce Wedges   Dressing
Rolls   Butter
Pudding Sundaes
or
Fruits in Nectar
Beverage

PREPARATION TIMETABLE

Start timing: Preheat oven
Assemble ingredients

At 5 minutes: Prepare Pudding Sundaes
or Fruits in Nectar

At 10 minutes: Prepare Ham in Stuffing
Shells

At 25 minutes: Heat canned beets
Cut lettuce wedges

At 30 minutes: Meal is ready to serve

Ham is excellent for speedy main dishes such as Ham in Stuffing Shells because most hams are fully cooked when purchased (check the label to make sure).

It will take you just a few minutes to heat the ham-vegetable mixture, leaving plenty of time to prepare the stuffing shells and the rest of the meal.

Pudding Sundaes

A fix-up for canned pudding—

Fold together one 17-ounce can chilled vanilla pudding; 1 cup dairy sour cream; and ¼ teaspoon almond extract. Spoon mixture into 6 sherbet dishes. Top *each* serving with 2 tablespoons apricot-pineapple preserves. Sprinkle *each* serving with about 1 tablespoon flaked coconut. Chill till served. Makes 6 servings.

Ham in Stuffing Shells

6 tablespoons butter or margarine
3 cups corn bread stuffing mix
1 slightly beaten egg
¼ cup water
• • •
2 8-ounce packages frozen mixed
vegetables with onion sauce
½ cup shredded sharp natural Cheddar
cheese (2 ounces)
2 cups cubed fully cooked ham

Preheat oven to 425°. Meanwhile, in saucepan melt butter. Remove from heat; add corn bread stuffing mix. Combine slightly beaten egg and water; add to butter-stuffing mixture in saucepan. Toss well to combine. Press stuffing mixture into bottom and up onto sides of 6 individual casseroles. Bake at 425° for 10 minutes.

Meanwhile, cook mixed vegetables with onion sauce according to package directions. Add shredded Cheddar cheese, stirring to melt. Add cubed ham; heat through. Spoon hot ham mixture into baked stuffing shells. Makes 6 servings.

Fruits in Nectar

½ teaspoon grated orange peel
½ cup orange juice
2 tablespoons cream sherry
1 tablespoon honey
1 29-ounce can fruits for salad,
drained

In saucepan combine first 4 ingredients; heat through, stirring occasionally. Cool slightly. Pour orange juice mixture over drained fruits. Serve warm. Garnish with fresh mint, if desired. Makes 6 servings.

An easy-to-prepare main dish

Serve everyone a hearty portion of tasty *Ham* → *in Stuffing Shells.* Bake the crispy stuffing shells while you heat the saucy ham-vegetable-cheese mixture atop the range.

SAUSAGE DINNER

Sausage Bourguignon
or
Pork Sausage Stroganoff
Hot Buttered Noodles
Buttered Green Beans
Pineapple-Cranberry Salad
Angel Cake
Beverage

PREPARATION TIMETABLE

Start timing: Assemble Ingredients

At 5 minutes: Prepare Pineapple-
Cranberry Salad

At 10 minutes: Prepare Sausage Bourguignon or Pork
Sausage Stroganoff

At 20 minutes: Cook noodles

At 25 minutes: Heat canned green beans

At 30 minutes: Meal is ready to serve

Sausage, which has long been a breakfast treat, will become a dinner favorite when you serve this menu. Sausage Bourguignon features brown-and-serve sausages in a creamy wine sauce, while Pork Sausage Stroganoff starts with bulk sausage and sour cream. Both are delicious over noodles.

Pineapple-Cranberry Salad

    1 8-ounce can whole cranberry sauce
    ¼ cup chopped walnuts
    ¼ cup chopped celery
    1 8-ounce can pineapple slices,
        drained (4 slices)
    Lettuce

Combine first 3 ingredients. Place each pineapple slice on lettuce-lined plate; spoon cranberry mixture over. Serves 4.

Sausage Bourguignon

Subtly flavored with Burgundy—

    1 8-ounce package brown-and-serve
        sausages
    ½ of a 10¾-ounce can beef gravy
        (⅔ cup)
    ½ cup light cream
    ¼ cup Burgundy
    2 tablespoons catsup
    1 tablespoon dried parsley flakes
    2 teaspoons cornstarch
    1 teaspoon instant minced onion
    ½ teaspoon Worcestershire sauce
    ⅛ teaspoon instant minced garlic

Cut brown-and-serve sausages into thirds. In medium skillet cook sausage pieces quickly till browned, turning often. Drain off excess fat. Combine beef gravy, light cream, Burgundy, catsup, dried parsley, cornstarch, instant minced onion, Worcestershire sauce, and instant minced garlic. Add to sausage in skillet; heat and stir just to boiling. Serve over hot buttered noodles. Makes 4 servings.

Pork Sausage Stroganoff

A delicious variation of an old favorite—

    1 pound bulk pork sausage
    ¼ cup fresh or frozen chopped onion
    3 tablespoons all-purpose flour
    1 teaspoon sugar
    1¼ cups water
    ½ cup tomato sauce
    1 3-ounce can sliced mushrooms,
        drained
    1 tablespoon instant beef bouillon
        granules
    1 cup dairy sour cream

In medium skillet cook sausage and onion over medium heat till sausage is lightly browned; drain off excess fat. Sprinkle flour and sugar over meat; blend in. Stir in water, tomato sauce, mushrooms, and bouillon granules. Simmer, uncovered, for 5 minutes. Stir in sour cream. Heat through, *but do not boil.* Serve over hot buttered noodles. Makes 4 servings.

STEAK DINNER

French Steak
Crunch-Top Potatoes
Buttered Brussels Sprouts
Spiced Peaches
Rolls   Butter
Angel Cake   Brittle Topping
Beverage

PREPARATION TIMETABLE

Start timing: Preheat oven
Assemble ingredients

At 5 minutes: Fix Crunch-Top Potatoes

At 10 minutes: Make Brittle Topping;
chill till served

At 15 minutes: Prepare French Steak

At 20 minutes: Cook Brussels sprouts

At 30 minutes: Meal is ready to serve

Two popular foods, steaks and onions, are combined in French Steak, the main dish of this menu. To prepare this simple dish, panfry the steak and then top with the cooked onion-wine mixture.

French Steak

In skillet cook 2 pounds beef sirloin steak, cut 1 inch thick, in 2 tablespoons cooking oil to desired doneness, turning once. Allow about 10 minutes for rare, 12 minutes for medium, and 20 minutes for well-done. Meanwhile, in saucepan cook 1 medium onion, sliced, in 2 tablespoons butter till tender. Stir in ½ cup dry white wine, 1 tablespoon Dijon-style mustard, and ⅛ teaspoon garlic powder; set aside. Remove steak to warm platter; skim excess fat from pan juices. Stir onion-wine mixture into pan juices, scraping pan; heat through. Serve with steak. Serves 6.

Crunch-Top Potatoes

¼ cup butter or margarine, melted
2 16-ounce cans sliced potatoes, drained
1 cup shredded natural Cheddar cheese (4 ounces)
¾ cup crushed cornflakes
1 teaspoon paprika

Preheat oven to 375°. Pour butter into 13x9x 2-inch baking pan. Add potatoes in single layer; turn once in butter. Mix remaining ingredients; sprinkle over potatoes. Bake at 375° about 20 minutes. Serves 6.

Brittle Topping

1 cup whipping cream
1 teaspoon vanilla
1 cup finely crushed peanut brittle, toffee, or peanut candy

Whip cream and vanilla to soft peaks; fold in candy. Serve over angel cake. Serves 6.

Slice *French Steak* thinly and then serve each person several of these slices and a generous portion of the onion-wine topping.

SEAFOOD DINNER

Medieval Shrimp
Hot Cooked Rice
Pea-Cheese Salad
or
Bean Toss
Buttered Carrots
Pound Cake   Frozen Strawberries
Beverage

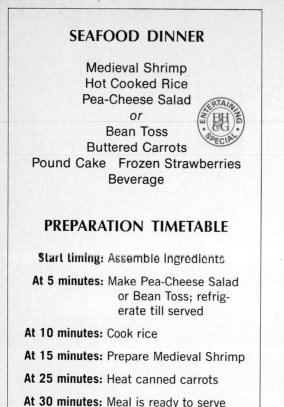

PREPARATION TIMETABLE

Start timing: Assemble Ingredients

At 5 minutes: Make Pea-Cheese Salad or Bean Toss; refrigerate till served

At 10 minutes: Cook rice

At 15 minutes: Prepare Medieval Shrimp

At 25 minutes: Heat canned carrots

At 30 minutes: Meal is ready to serve

The delicate flavor of shrimp is delightfully complemented with a dill-butter mixture in Medieval Shrimp. To make this dish extra-special, use shrimp in shells and let your guests peel them at the table.

Pea-Cheese Salad

>   1 16-ounce can peas, chilled and drained
> ½ cup cubed natural Cheddar cheese
>   2 tablespoons chopped canned pimiento
> ⅓ cup thousand island salad dressing
> Dash onion powder
> Lettuce

Combine first 3 ingredients. Mix salad dressing and onion powder; toss lightly with pea-cheese mixture. Serve on lettuce-lined plates. Makes 4 servings.

Medieval Shrimp

>   1 12-ounce can beer (1½ cups)
> ¼ teaspoon salt
> ¼ teaspoon celery salt
> ⅛ teaspoon onion powder
>   3 pounds fresh or frozen shrimp in shells *or* 1½ pounds frozen shelled shrimp
> ¼ cup butter or margarine
>   1 tablespoon lemon juice
> ½ teaspoon dried dillweed, crushed

In large saucepan bring first 4 ingredients to a boil. Add shrimp. Heat to boiling; reduce heat and simmer till shrimp turn pink, 2 to 3 minutes. Drain. Meanwhile, in small saucepan melt butter. Stir in lemon juice and dillweed. Serve hot butter mixture with shrimp. Makes 4 servings.

Bean Toss

In salad bowl combine 3 cups torn lettuce; one 15½-ounce can chilled French-style green beans, drained; and 3 tablespoons grated Parmesan cheese. Toss with enough Italian salad dressing to coat. Serves 4.

For your next dinner party serve *Medieval Shrimp.* Cook shrimp in a beer mixture, then serve with a tasty dill butter.

LAMB DINNER

Lamb Chop-Potato Broil
Lettuce Wedges
with
Zesty Dressing *or* Rosé Dressing
Buttered Asparagus
Canned Fruit
Beverage

PREPARATION TIMETABLE

Start timing: Preheat broiler
Assemble ingredients

At 5 minutes: Prepare Zesty Dressing
or Rosé Dressing and
lettuce wedges; re-
frigerate till served

At 12 minutes: Prepare Lamb Chop-
Potato Broil

At 20 minutes: Cook frozen asparagus

At 30 minutes: Meal is ready to serve

Thanks to your broiler, you can have this meal ready in no time. First, while the broiler preheats, prepare the salad dressing and lettuce. Then, broil the main dish. As this broils, you'll have time to prepare the sour cream topping for the chops, and cook the asparagus.

Zesty Dressing

1 package creamy Russian salad
dressing mix
2/3 cup tomato juice
1/4 cup vinegar
1 tablespoon salad oil

In screw-top jar combine creamy Russian salad dressing mix, tomato juice, vinegar, and salad oil; cover and shake well. Chill till served. Makes 1 cup dressing.

Lamb Chop-Potato Broil

The meat and potatoes broil side-by-side—

4 lamb shoulder chops
2 16-ounce cans whole new potatoes,
drained
2 tablespoons butter or margarine
1 tablespoon lemon juice
1 teaspoon dried parsley flakes
1/2 teaspoon instant minced onion
Dash pepper
Dash ground nutmeg
• • •
1/2 cup dairy sour cream
1 tablespoon all-purpose flour
1 3-ounce can sliced mushrooms,
drained
1/4 cup milk
1 teaspoon instant minced onion
1/4 teaspoon dried thyme, crushed

Preheat broiler. Place lamb chops on un-heated broiler pan. Place potatoes in foil pan beside chops. Broil 3 to 4 inches from heat for 7 to 8 minutes. Meanwhile, melt butter. Blend in lemon juice, dried parsley, 1/2 teaspoon instant minced onion, pepper, and ground nutmeg; heat through. Pour butter mixture over potatoes; turn lamb chops. Broil 6 to 7 minutes more.

Meanwhile, in small saucepan combine dairy sour cream and flour. Stir in sliced mushrooms, milk, 1 teaspoon instant minced onion, and crushed thyme. Heat through, *but do not boil.* To serve, spoon sour cream mixture over lamb chops. Serves 4.

Rosé Dressing

An easy-to-make wine salad dressing—

1/2 cup rosé
1/2 cup Russian salad dressing
1/2 package dry Italian salad dressing
mix (2 teaspoons)
1 tablespoon grated Parmesan cheese

In screw-top jar combine rosé, Russian salad dressing, dry Italian dressing mix, and grated Parmesan cheese. Cover tightly and shake to mix. Shake again just before serv-ing. Makes about 1 cup dressing.

<table>
<tr><td>

FAMILY DINNER

Stroganoff Meatballs
or
Oriental-Style Meatballs
or
Deviled Meatballs
Buttered Mixed Vegetables
Spiced Apple Rings
Angel Cake with Lemon-Yogurt
Topping
or
Pound Cake with Tutti-Frutti Topping
Beverage

PREPARATION TIMETABLE

Start timing: Assemble ingredients

At 5 minutes: Cook rice pilaf or rice
Prepare Lemon-Yogurt
Topping or Tutti-
Frutti Topping

At 12 minutes: Make Stroganoff Meat-
balls or Oriental-
Style Meatballs or
Deviled Meatballs

At 25 minutes: Heat canned vegetables

At 30 minutes: Meal is ready to serve

</td></tr>
</table>

Do you find yourself serving the same old family favorites again and again? If so, try these tempting, jiffy recipes and add variety to your list of meal favorites.

Meatballs are ready in minutes when you prepare Stroganoff Meatballs, Oriental-Style Meatballs, or Deviled Meatballs. Just add extra ingredients to canned meatballs in gravy to create these tasty main dishes. Served over generous portions of hot cooked rice or rice pilaf, they will satisfy even the most hearty appetites. For dessert, top slices of purchased angel cake or pound cake with spoonfuls of tangy Lemon-Yogurt Topping or fruit-filled Tutti-Frutti Topping.

Stroganoff Meatballs

    2 12-ounce packages frozen rice
        pilaf
    1 medium onion, sliced
    2 tablespoons butter or margarine
    2 15-ounce cans meatballs in gravy
    1 6-ounce can sliced mushrooms,
        drained
    ¾ cup dairy sour cream
    2 tablespoons snipped parsley
        (optional)

Prepare rice pilaf according to package directions. Meanwhile, cook onion in butter till tender but not brown. Add meatballs in gravy and the mushrooms; bring to boiling. Reduce heat and simmer 5 minutes. Blend some of the hot gravy into sour cream; return to remaining hot mixture in saucepan. Heat through, *but do not boil.* Serve over hot pilaf. Sprinkle with snipped parsley, if desired. Makes 8 servings.

Deviled Meatballs

    2 15-ounce cans meatballs in gravy
    ½ cup bottled barbecue sauce with
        onion
    1 teaspoon Worcestershire sauce
    ½ teaspoon dry mustard
    ¼ teaspoon instant minced garlic
        Hot cooked rice

Combine first 5 ingredients. Bring to a boil; simmer 5 minutes. Serve mixture over hot cooked rice. Makes 8 servings.

Lemon-Yogurt Topping

    1 3¾-ounce package *instant* lemon
        pudding mix
    1½ cups milk
    1 cup plain or lemon yogurt

Prepare lemon pudding according to package directions, *except* use the 1½ cups milk. Stir in the plain or lemon yogurt. Chill mixture till served. Serve over angel cake slices. Makes 8 servings.

Set the mood for a warm and appealing family dinner with easy *Stroganoff Meatballs*. Serve this tasty combination of meatballs, sour cream, and mushrooms in thick gravy over hot rice pilaf.

Oriental-Style Meatballs

1 13½-ounce can pineapple tidbits
⅓ cup packed brown sugar
3 tablespoons cornstarch
⅛ teaspoon ground ginger
⅓ cup vinegar
1 tablespoon soy sauce
2 15-ounce cans meatballs in gravy
1 16-ounce can fancy mixed Chinese
    vegetables
Hot cooked rice

Drain pineapple; reserve syrup. Add water to syrup to make 1 cup. Combine brown sugar, cornstarch, and ginger; blend in syrup-water mixture. Add vinegar and soy sauce. Cook and stir till thickened. Stir in meatballs in gravy, Chinese vegetables, and pineapple. Bring to boiling, stirring occasionally. Serve over hot rice. Serves 8.

Tutti-Frutti Topping

This fluffy topping is filled with pieces of maraschino cherries, sliced bananas, and coconut. Next time, try it on ice cream—

2 medium bananas
1½ cups frozen whipped topping,
    thawed
⅓ cup flaked coconut
¼ cup sliced maraschino cherries,
    well drained
Few drops almond extract

Peel and slice bananas. In mixing bowl fold together thawed whipped topping, sliced bananas, flaked coconut, well-drained maraschino cherries, and a few drops almond extract. Chill topping-fruit mixture until served. To serve, generously spoon topping-fruit mixture over slices of pound cake. Makes 8 servings.

HAM DINNER

Ham-Fruit Combo
Individual Potato Bakes
Vegetable Toss
or
Torn Greens   Jiffy Dressing
Canned Chocolate Pudding
Beverage

PREPARATION TIMETABLE

Start timing: Preheat oven
Assemble ingredients

At 5 minutes: Prepare Individual
Potato Bakes; bake

At 12 minutes: Prepare Vegetable Toss
or Jiffy Dressing and
torn greens

At 18 minutes: Prepare Ham-Fruit Combo

At 30 minutes: Meal is ready to serve

Need a quick and easy dinner to prepare after a hectic day? Try this one. Bake the potatoes in the oven while you prepare the vegetable salad or dressing. Then, finish up by browning the ham and fruit in an electric skillet. Your family won't have to wait long for this hearty meal.

Ham-Fruit Combo

1 1½-pound fully cooked ham slice
1 16-ounce can peach halves, drained
1 16-ounce can pear halves, drained
2 tablespoons butter or margarine

Preheat electric skillet to 340°. Brown ham slice slowly on both sides, about 4 minutes for *each* side. Place peaches and pears around ham in skillet. Dot fruit with butter. Brown the fruit, turning once, about 4 minutes. Makes 6 servings.

Individual Potato Bakes

Prepare these tangy potato casseroles using instant mashed potatoes and sour cream—

Packaged instant mashed potatoes
(enough for 4 servings)
½ cup dairy sour cream
1 teaspoon dried parsley flakes
¼ teaspoon onion salt

Preheat oven to 375°. Prepare instant mashed potatoes according to the package directions. Stir sour cream, dried parsley flakes, and onion salt into prepared potatoes. Spoon potato mixture into six individual casseroles or custard cups. Bake at 375° till heated through and lightly browned, about 15 minutes. Serves 6.

Vegetable Toss

1 medium head lettuce, torn
into bite-sized pieces
½ medium cucumber, sliced
½ of a 3½-ounce can French-fried
onions
¼ cup grated Parmesan cheese
½ cup thousand island salad dressing

In salad bowl combine lettuce, cucumber, French-fried onions, and cheese. Chill till served. Before serving, drizzle lettuce mixture with thousand island dressing; toss lightly. Makes 6 servings.

Jiffy Dressing

Turn bottled dressings into a flavor treat—

½ cup green goddess salad dressing
½ cup dairy sour cream
¼ cup Caesar salad dressing
2 tablespoons lemon juice
¼ cup bacon-flavored protein bits

In small bowl stir together green goddess salad dressing, dairy sour cream, Caesar salad dressing, and lemon juice; chill till served. Just before serving, stir in bacon flavored protein bits *or* sprinkle them atop salad. Makes 1¼ cups dressing.

Land and Sea Broil

Broil 6 beef top loin steaks, cut ½ inch thick, about 3 inches from heat for 8 to 10 minutes; turn once. Pile ⅙ *of one* 5-ounce can lobster, drained, broken in pieces, and cartilage removed, *atop each.* Cut 3 slices process Swiss cheese in half diagonally; top *each* steak with one triangle. Broil till cheese melts. Serves 6.

Pineapple Jubilee

Combine ½ cup orange marmalade and 2 tablespoons *each* packed brown sugar and light corn syrup. Add one 13½-ounce can pineapple tidbits, drained. Cook and stir till hot. Heat ¼ cup orange-flavored liqueur; ignite and pour over fruit mixture. Spoon over vanilla ice cream. Serves 6.

Set *Pineapple Jubilee* aflame at the table for a spectacular dinner finale. Your guests will love this simple, yet elegant fruit sauce.

SUNDAY DINNER

Land and Sea Broil
Instant Mashed Potatoes
Buttered Asparagus
Hard Rolls   Butter
Spiced Peaches
Pineapple Jubilee
Beverage

(ENTERTAINING BH&G SPECIAL)

PREPARATION TIMETABLE

Start timing: Preheat broiler
Assemble ingredients

At 5 minutes: Combine ingredients for Pineapple Jubilee sauce; set aside

At 15 minutes: Broil steak for Land and Sea Broil

At 20 minutes: Cook frozen asparagus Scoop ice cream; freeze till served

At 25 minutes: Add crab and cheese to Land and Sea Broil Prepare instant mashed potatoes

At 30 minutes: Meal is ready to serve Heat Pineapple Jubilee sauce when served

Invite special friends for Sunday dinner when your menu features elegant Land and Sea Broil—steak topped with lobster and Swiss cheese. To round out the meal in style, serve flaming Pineapple Jubilee. If you have a chafing dish, now is the perfect time to use it. Bring the chafing dish to the table and heat the sauce in the blazer pan. Then, keep it warm over hot water (bain-marie). To flame, heat orange-flavored liqueur in a ladle or small pan. Then, while your guests watch, ignite the spirits and pour over the pineapple mixture. When the flame dies, a subtle liqueur flavor will remain.

Suppers

FONDUE SUPPER

Beer Rarebit Fondue
or
Swiss-Cheese Fondue
or
Chili Fondue
Spinach Toss *or* Fruit-Greens Toss
Canned Fruit   Angel Cake
Beverage

PREPARATION TIMETABLE

Start timing: Assemble ingredients

At 5 minutes: Prepare Spinach Toss or
Fruit-Greens Toss;
chill till served

At 12 minutes: Cut French bread into
pieces for fondue

At 15 minutes: Fix Beer Rarebit Fondue
or Swiss Cheese Fon-
due or Chili Fondue

At 30 minutes: Meal is ready to serve

Looking for an easy menu for entertaining? Here's one that gives a choice of three variations of cheese fondue.

To avoid last-minute rush, prepare the salad first and keep it refrigerated until mealtime. Next, make one of these easy-to-prepare fondues and the party's ready to begin. Set out the fondue pots and let your guests fondue at the table.

Remember, one large loaf of French bread makes enough dippers for 6 to 8 people. If the fondue becomes too thick, try warming and adding a little of the liquid called for in the recipe. Now, dip into the fondue and enjoy the party mood.

Swiss Cheese Fondue

3 tablespoons thinly sliced green
onion with tops
1 tablespoon butter or margarine
2 teaspoons all-purpose flour
3 cups shredded process Swiss
cheese (12 ounces)
1½ cups dairy sour cream
½ cup milk
¼ teaspoon ground nutmeg
French bread, cut in bite-size
pieces, each with one crust

In saucepan cook green onion in butter or margarine till tender but not brown. Stir in flour. Add process Swiss cheese, dairy sour cream, milk, and ground nutmeg. Cook over low heat, stirring constantly, till cheese is melted. Transfer to fondue pot; place over fondue burner. Spear French bread cube with fondue fork; dip into fondue mixture. Makes 6 servings.

Chili Fondue

2 10½-ounce cans chili without beans
1 cup shredded sharp process
American cheese (4 ounces)
½ to 1 teaspoon chili powder
⅓ cup dry wine or cold water
1 tablespoon cornstarch
French bread, cut in bite-size
pieces, each with one crust
or frankfurter pieces

In medium saucepan combine chili without beans, American cheese, and chili powder; stir over low heat till cheese is melted. Blend together wine or water and cornstarch; add to chili-cheese mixture. Cook and stir till thickened and bubbly. Transfer to fondue pot; place over fondue burner. Spear bread cube or frankfurter piece with fondue fork; dip in fondue mixture, swirling to coat. Makes 6 servings.

Beer Rarebit Fondue

    4 cups shredded sharp natural
        Cheddar cheese (16 ounces)
  ½ cup beer
  1 tablespoon cornstarch
  ½ teaspoon dry mustard
  ⅛ teaspoon garlic powder
  1 teaspoon Worcestershire sauce
    Dash bottled hot pepper sauce
    French bread, cut in bite-size
      pieces, each with one crust

Have cheese at room temperature. In heavy saucepan heat beer slowly. Coat cheese with cornstarch, mustard, and garlic powder; add Worcestershire and hot pepper sauce. Gradually add cheese to beer, stirring constantly over medium-low heat till cheese is melted. (Do not allow mixture to become too hot.) Transfer to fondue pot; place over fondue burner. Spear a bread cube with fondue fork. Dip into fondue and swirl to coat bread. Makes 6 servings.

Spinach Toss

Lemon juice adds zip to this spinach salad—

  6 cups torn spinach
  1 cup sliced fresh mushrooms
  1 cup halved cherry tomatoes
  ½ teaspoon salt
    Dash freshly ground pepper
  ¼ cup salad oil
  2 tablespoons lemon juice

Wash and drain spinach on paper toweling. Arrange in salad bowl with mushrooms and cherry tomatoes. Sprinkle with salt and pepper. Combine oil and lemon juice; toss with salad. Makes 6 servings.

Fruit-Greens Toss

In salad bowl combine 3 cups torn lettuce; 3 cups torn curly endive; one 11-ounce can mandarin orange sections, drained; and 1 small onion, sliced and separated into rings. At serving time, toss lightly with ⅓ cup Italian salad dressing. Serves 6.

Cheddar cheese and beer combine to make this creamy *Beer Rarebit Fondue.* Garlic and hot pepper seasoning are unexpected flavor bonuses.

PIZZA SUPPER

Pizza-Rama
or
Seashore Pizza
or
Pizza Mexicano
Torn Greens   Creamy Dressing
Ice Cream
Beverage

PREPARATION TIMETABLE

Start timing: Preheat oven
                 Assemble ingredients

At 5 minutes: Prepare Pizza-Rama or
                  Seashore Pizza or
                  Pizza Mexicano

At 15 minutes: Bake pizza
                   Tear greens

At 20 minutes: Prepare Creamy Dressing

At 30 minutes: Meal is ready to serve

You'll please every member of your family with any one of these three taste-tempting pizza recipes. Whichever you select, Pizza Supper is quick and easy because you start with frozen cheese pizzas.

Pizza Mexicano

2 12-inch frozen cheese pizzas
  Chili powder
1 4½-ounce can chopped ripe olives
1 4-ounce can chopped green chilies
1 cup shredded natural Monterey Jack
  cheese (4 ounces)

Sprinkle *each* frozen cheese pizza with chili powder, *half* the ripe olives, *half* the green chilies, and *half* the Monterey Jack cheese. Bake according to package directions. Makes 4 servings.

Pizza-Rama

This tasty pizza is shown on page 8 —

½ cup fresh or frozen chopped green
  pepper
½ cup fresh or frozen chopped onion
1 tablespoon cooking oil
2 12-inch frozen cheese pizzas
  Dried oregano, crushed
2 ounces sliced pepperoni
1 3-ounce can chopped mushrooms,
  drained
1 cup shredded natural mozzarella
  cheese (4 ounces)

Cook green pepper and onion in oil. Sprinkle *each* pizza lightly with oregano. Sprinkle green pepper and onion over *half of each* pizza. Arrange pepperoni and mushrooms over *other half of each* pizza. Sprinkle cheese over all. Bake pizzas according to package directions. Serves 4.

Seashore Pizza

2 12-inch frozen cheese pizzas
1 8-ounce can tomato sauce with
  cheese
  Dried oregano, crushed
2 7½-ounce cans minced clams,
  drained *or* 2 2-ounce cans
  anchovies
½ cup grated Parmesan cheese

Spread *each* pizza with *half* of the tomato sauce with cheese. Sprinkle with oregano. Top *each* with *half* clams *or* anchovies; sprinkle with Parmesan. Bake pizzas according to package directions. Serves 4.

Creamy Dressing

½ cup dairy sour cream
½ cup Russian salad dressing
2 tablespoons sliced pimiento-
  stuffed green olives

Combine sour cream and Russian salad dressing; mix well. Stir in olives. Serve over torn greens. Makes 1 cup dressing.

While your husband picks up the chicken, prepare the salad, beans, and dessert fondue for this family-pleasing supper. Serve one salad and dessert tonight, and prepare the other choices another time.

Chocolate-Nut Fondue

Combine one 6-ounce package semisweet chocolate pieces, ½ cup sugar, and ½ cup milk. Cook and stir till chocolate melts. Blend in ½ cup chunk-style peanut butter. Pour the mixture into fondue pot; place over fondue burner. Dip angel cake cubes. Makes 6 servings.

Dairy Garden Salad

Use fresh tomatoes, radishes, and onions—

  1 cup large-curd, cream-style cottage cheese
  ½ cup dairy sour cream
  ¼ cup sliced radishes
  ¼ cup sliced green onion
  ⅛ teaspoon salt
  6 tomato slices

Blend cottage cheese with dairy sour cream. Stir in radishes, green onion, salt, and dash pepper. To serve, spoon over tomato slices. Makes 6 servings.

Ginger-Melon Salad

Ginger and orange marmalade combine to accent the flavor of fresh cantaloupe—

  1 cup dairy sour cream
  ¼ cup orange marmalade
  ¼ teaspoon ground ginger
  1 small cantaloupe, seeded, peeled, and sliced

Combine dairy sour cream, orange marmalade, and ground ginger. Serve over cantaloupe slices. Makes 6 servings.

Frosting Mix Fondue

  1 package coconut-almond *or* coconut-pecan frosting mix (for 2-layer cake)
  ½ cup nonfat dry milk powder
  1 to 1¼ cups water
  ¼ cup butter or margarine
    Angel cake, cut in bite-size pieces

In small saucepan combine coconut-almond *or* coconut-pecan frosting mix and milk powder. Stir in ¼ *cup* water. Add butter or margarine; heat and stir till butter melts. Add enough of the remaining water to make mixture of dipping consistency. Pour into fondue pot; place over fondue burner. Spear angel cake cube with fondue fork; dip into fondue. Makes 6 servings.

Ski slopes are great places for making friends, and when the day ends, you'll want to keep those friendships alive over a cozy supper. Hungry skiers are easy to satisfy when you prepare this menu featuring Hearty Fiesta Burgers. If your party is larger than expected, it's easy to make extra since the ingredients are common ones that can be kept on hand. Round out the meal with steaming hot mugs of Spicy Buttered Lemonade.

Winter warm-up menu

← Follow up a day of skiing or any other winter activity with slices of *Parsley-Buttered Loaf, Spicy Buttered Lemonade,* cheese-topped *Hearty Fiesta Burgers,* and chocolate brownies.

Hearty Fiesta Burgers

¾ cup fine saltine cracker crumbs
2 eggs
¼ cup catsup
2 teaspoons instant minced onion
2 teaspoons Worcestershire sauce
1 pound ground beef
1 10½-ounce can condensed cream of
mushroom soup
1 15-ounce can kidney beans, drained
⅓ cup fresh or frozen chopped green
pepper
½ cup shredded natural Cheddar
cheese (2 ounces)

Combine first 5 ingredients, ¼ teaspoon salt, and dash pepper. Add meat and mix well; shape into 6 patties. In large skillet brown the patties on both sides. Pour soup over meat; top with beans and green pepper. Cook, covered, over low heat 10 minutes. Sprinkle with cheese; cover and heat till cheese melts. Makes 6 servings.

Parsley-Buttered Loaf

Bake 1 loaf brown-and-serve bread with pull-apart slices according to package directions. Meanwhile, combine ¼ cup softened butter, 1 tablespoon snipped parsley, and ¼ teaspoon onion salt. Split bread halfway down along each separation; spread butter mixture between. Serves 6.

Spicy Buttered Lemonade

2 6-ounce cans frozen lemonade
concentrate
1 teaspoon whole cloves
1 inch stick cinnamon
2 tablespoons butter or margarine

Combine lemonade and 5 cups water. Tie cloves and stick cinnamon in cheesecloth bag; add to lemonade mixture. Bring to boiling; reduce heat and simmer 5 minutes. Remove spices. Pour into mugs; top *each* with 1 teaspoon butter. Serve with cinnamon stick stirrers, if desired. Serves 6.

SKILLET SUPPER

Pecos-Style Frankfurters
or
Chili Burger Supper
Buttered Green Beans
Orange-Topped Cake
or
Ice Cream   Mincemeat Sauce
Beverage

PREPARATION TIMETABLE

Start timing: Heat broiler, if needed
Assemble ingredients

At 5 minutes: Prepare Pecos-Style
Frankfurters or Chili
Burger Supper

At 15 minutes: Make Orange-Topped Cake
or Mincemeat Sauce

At 20 minutes: Heat canned green beans

At 25 minutes: Meal is ready to serve

Prepare Pecos-Style Frankfurters or Chili Burger Supper for an easy, one-skillet meal. While the main dish cooks, prepare the dessert and heat the vegetable.

Chili Burger Supper

1 cup elbow macaroni (4 ounces)
1 pound ground beef
1 11-ounce can condensed chili-beef
    soup
1 10¾-ounce can condensed tomato
    soup
3 slices sharp process American
    cheese, halved (3 ounces)

Cook macaroni; drain. Meanwhile, brown meat; drain off fat. Add soups and macaroni; heat and stir till bubbly. Top with cheese. Cover; heat till melted. Serves 6.

Pecos-Style Frankfurters

1 16-ounce can whole kernel corn
1 8-ounce can tomato sauce
1 6-ounce package instant Spanish
    rice mix
1 cup water
½ cup sliced ripe olives
1 teaspoon instant chicken bouillon
    granules
• • •
6 frankfurters, scored diagonally

In 10-inch skillet combine undrained whole kernel corn, tomato sauce, Spanish rice mix, water, sliced ripe olives, and chicken bouillon granules. Bring to boiling. Top mixture with frankfurters; cover and cook over low heat till rice is done, about 12 minutes. Makes 6 servings.

Orange-Topped Cake

½ cup orange marmalade
2 teaspoons lemon juice
⅔ cup flaked coconut
⅔ cup miniature marshmallows
• • •
6 slices pound cake

Preheat broiler. Combine orange marmalade and lemon juice. Stir in flaked coconut and miniature marshmallows; spread on pound cake slices. Broil cake 3 to 4 inches from heat till marshmallows are golden brown, about 1 minute. Serves 6.

Mincemeat Sauce

1 cup prepared mincemeat
¼ cup chopped pecans
¼ cup sliced maraschino cherries
¼ cup light corn syrup
2 tablespoons orange-flavored
    breakfast drink powder

Combine prepared mincemeat, pecans, maraschino cherries, corn syrup, and orange-flavored breakfast drink powder. Serve over vanilla ice cream. Makes 1½ cups.

Have you run out of ideas for feeding the hearty eaters in your family? If so, try this simple and filling supper menu. They're sure to like it.

Raisin-Rice Pudding

¾ cup uncooked packaged precooked
    rice
¾ cup water
½ cup raisins
1¾ cups milk
1 3- to 3¼-ounce package *regular*
    vanilla pudding mix
½ teaspoon vanilla
    Ground cinnamon or nutmeg

In saucepan combine rice, water, and raisins. Bring to boiling; cover and simmer 4 minutes. Stir in milk and pudding mix. Cook and stir over medium-high heat till thickened and bubbly. Remove from heat. Add vanilla. Sprinkle with ground cinnamon or nutmeg. Serve warm. Makes 6 servings.

Bologna Bunwiches

Cook ½ cup fresh or frozen chopped green pepper in 2 tablespoons cooking oil till tender. Stir in one 8-ounce can kidney beans, drained; one 8-ounce can tomato sauce; 6 ounces bologna, cut in strips; 1 tablespoon instant minced onion; and 1 teaspoon chili powder. Heat through. Stir in ½ cup shredded natural Cheddar cheese; heat till cheese melts. Serve in 6 frankfurter buns, split and toasted. Serves 6.

Tapioca Fluff

Into one 17-ounce can tapioca pudding fold 1 cup frozen whipped topping, thawed; ¼ cup flaked coconut; and 10 quartered maraschino cherries. Spoon into serving dishes; chill till served. Serves 6.

Fill toasted buns with mixture of kidney beans, bologna, and tomato sauce to make tasty *Bologna Bunwiches.* Serve with mugs of iced tea.

If you're like most homemakers, you spend most of the meal preparation time on the main dish. So, when you're in a hurry, it makes sense to select a fast main dish.

In this section you'll find 101 main dish recipes with one thing in common—they are all quick to prepare. There are shortcut recipes for family favorites such as meat loaf and chicken and noodles, elegant dishes such as chicken curry and sole en papillote, casseroles, skillet dishes, saucepan dishes, soups, broiled entrées, main dish salads, and hearty sandwiches that are a meal by themselves. And to make the best use of leftovers, particularly meats, try the recipes on pages 76 and 77.

Just choose any of these tasty recipes and you're on your way to spending less time in the kitchen.

Fast Main Dishes

For a fancy, easy-to-prepare luncheon or supper main dish, serve *Ham Sandwich Deluxe*. This sandwich starts with a rye bread loaf and packaged ham salad.

From the Oven

Ham and Cauliflower Casserole

    2 10-ounce packages frozen
        cauliflower
    2 tablespoons butter or margarine
    2 tablespoons all-purpose flour
    ½ teaspoon salt
        Dash pepper
    1 cup milk
    2 teaspoons instant minced onion
    ½ cup shredded sharp natural
        Cheddar cheese (2 ounces)
    2 cups cubed fully cooked ham
    1 3-ounce can sliced mushrooms,
        drained
    5 saltine crackers, crumbled
    1 tablespoon butter or margarine,
        melted

Preheat oven to 350°. In medium saucepan cook cauliflower according to package directions. Drain well. Meanwhile, in large saucepan melt 2 tablespoons butter. Stir in flour, salt, and pepper; add milk and onion. Cook and stir till thickened and bubbly; stir in cheese till melted. Gently fold in ham, mushrooms, and cauliflower. Turn into 1½-quart casserole. Combine crackers and 1 tablespoon melted butter; sprinkle on top. Bake at 350° till heated through, about 15 minutes. Serves 6.

Scalloped Chicken

Old-fashioned recipe made in a hurry —

Preheat oven to 350°. In large bowl combine 2 cups herb-seasoned stuffing mix; 2 cups cubed cooked chicken; ¼ cup chopped celery leaves; ¼ cup butter, melted; and 1 tablespoon instant minced onion.

   In saucepan combine one 10½-ounce can condensed cream of mushroom soup and ¾ cup water; heat through. Pour over stuffing mixture. Mix well. Spoon into individual casseroles. Bake at 350° till heated through, about 15 minutes. Serves 4.

Fillet of Sole en Papillote

    1 envelope white sauce mix (enough
        for 1 cup sauce)
    1 4½-ounce can shrimp, drained
    1 3-ounce can sliced mushrooms,
        drained
    ½ teaspoon Worcestershire sauce
    ¼ teaspoon paprika
    4 frozen sole fillets,
        thawed
    1 tablespoon snipped parsley

Preheat oven to 400°. Prepare sauce according to package directions. Stir in next 4 ingredients. Slit 4 unwaxed paper lunch sacks* lengthwise. On *each* sack place one sole fillet; top *each* with ¼ of the shrimp mixture. Close slits with paper clips; fold ends under. Bake on baking sheet at 400° for 20 minutes. Garnish with parsley. Serves 4.

   *Or, use eight 14x12-inch pieces of foil. Place fish and shrimp mixture on 4 of the pieces. Cover with remaining foil; seal.

Chicken-Noodle Bake

Preheat oven to 375°. Mix one 15¼-ounce can chicken and noodles in gravy; one 8½-ounce can peas, drained; one 5-ounce can boned chicken, cut up; one 3-ounce can chopped mushrooms, drained; and ¼ teaspoon dried thyme, crushed. Put into 9-inch pie plate. Mix 5 rich round crackers, crumbled, and 1 tablespoon butter, melted; sprinkle over. Bake at 375° for 20 minutes. Makes 4 servings.

Fast gourmet speciality

Before serving elegant *Fillet of Sole en Papillote,* open up individual packets and sprinkle with snipped parsley. This entrée consists of sole smothered with a shrimp and mushroom sauce.

Easy Cheesy Soufflé

2 tablespoons butter or margarine
1 tablespoon fine dry bread crumbs
3 tablespoons all-purpose flour
    Dash pepper
    Dash ground nutmeg
1 cup milk
1 5-ounce jar process cheese
    spread with bacon
3 egg whites
3 slightly beaten egg yolks

Preheat oven to 400°. Meanwhile, grease bottom and sides of a 5-cup soufflé dish with *1 tablespoon* of the butter; sprinkle with bread crumbs. Melt remaining butter; blend in flour, pepper, and nutmeg. Add milk all at once, and cook and stir till thickened and bubbly. Add cheese spread; stir over low heat till cheese melts.

Beat egg whites till stiff but not dry; set aside. Add a little of hot mixture to yolks; return to remaining hot mixture. Cook, stirring constantly, till thickened, about 1 minute; remove from heat. Fold in stiffly beaten whites. Turn into prepared soufflé dish. Bake at 400° till golden brown and puffy, 23 to 25 minutes. Serve immediately. Makes 4 servings.

Muffin Pan Meat Loaves

Each person gets three little meat loaves—

1 8-ounce can tomato sauce
1 cup herb-seasoned stuffing mix
1 slightly beaten egg
1 teaspoon salt
¼ teaspoon pepper
1½ pounds ground beef
¼ cup catsup
2 tablespoons brown sugar
1 tablespoon vinegar
½ teaspoon dry mustard

Preheat oven to 350°. Meanwhile, combine first 5 ingredients. Add ground beef; mix well. Spoon mixture into 18 muffin cups. Combine remaining ingredients; spread over top of meat loaves. Bake at 350° for 25 minutes. Makes 6 servings.

Spanish Rice Loaves

1 pound ground beef
1 8-ounce can Spanish rice (1 cup)
1 egg
2 tablespoons instant minced onion
½ teaspoon salt

Preheat oven to 350°. Meanwhile, mix beef, Spanish rice, egg, onion, and salt. Shape into 4 individual loaves. Bake on baking sheet at 350° for 35 minutes. Serves 4.

Meat and Potato Pie

Packaged instant mashed potatoes
    (enough for 8 servings)
1 cup milk
1 slightly beaten egg
¼ cup catsup
1 tablespoon instant minced onion
¾ teaspoon salt
⅛ teaspoon pepper
1 pound ground beef

• • •

½ cup shredded sharp natural Cheddar
    cheese (2 ounces)

Preheat oven to 350°. Meanwhile, combine *half of the dry* instant mashed potatoes, milk, slightly beaten egg, catsup, onion, salt, and pepper. Add beef and mix well. Spread in 9-inch pie plate. Bake at 350° about 35 minutes. Prepare remaining potatoes according to package directions; spoon atop hot pie. Sprinkle cheese over potatoes. Bake 3 to 4 minutes more. Cut in wedges; serve with additional catsup, if desired. Makes 4 or 5 servings.

Hash Crowns

Preheat oven to 375°. Remove both ends of a 16-ounce can chilled corned beef hash; push out hash. Cut into 4 slices; top *each* slice with a drained pineapple slice from one 8½-ounce can sliced pineapple. Fill pineapple centers with ¼ cup whole cranberry sauce. Bake in shallow baking dish at 375° for 20 minutes. Serves 4.

Corn Puff Ham Sandwiches

Egg mixture forms a puffy crown—

    4 English muffins or hamburger buns
    1 4½-ounce can deviled ham
    1 8¾-ounce can whole kernel corn,
        well drained
    ¼ teaspoon salt
        • • •
    3 egg yolks
    ½ teaspoon prepared mustard
    ½ cup shredded process American
        cheese (2 ounces)
    3 egg whites

Preheat oven to 375°. Split and toast muffins or buns. Spread each half with deviled ham. Combine corn and salt; spread evenly over ham. Beat egg yolks and mustard till thick and lemon-colored; fold in shredded cheese. Beat egg whites till stiff but not dry. Gradually fold beaten whites into yolk mixture. Spoon onto muffins, spreading just to edges. Place on ungreased baking sheet; bake at 375° till golden, 12 to 15 minutes. Makes 4 servings.

No-Crust Pizzas

A new way to prepare a favorite dish—

    1 8-ounce can pizza sauce (1 cup)
    1 slightly beaten egg
    ¼ cup fine dry bread crumbs
    ¼ cup fresh or frozen chopped
        onion
    1 medium clove garlic, minced
    ¾ teaspoon salt
    1½ pounds ground beef
    1 cup shredded natural mozzarella
        cheese (4 ounces)

Preheat oven to 450°. Combine ¼ *cup* of the pizza sauce, egg, crumbs, onion, garlic, and salt. Add meat and mix well. Divide into six portions. On foil-lined 15½x10½x1-inch baking pan, shape each portion to 3½-inch circle, building up a ¾-inch rim. (Be sure rim is high enough to contain sauce.) Spoon remaining sauce atop meat. Bake at 450° for 10 minutes. Top with cheese; bake 5 minutes more. Serves 6.

Surprise Turnovers

The meat filling is the surprise—

    2 packages refrigerated crescent
        rolls (16 rolls)
    1 12-ounce can luncheon meat
    1 tablespoon prepared mustard
    2 teaspoons snipped parsley
      Milk
        • • •
    1 20-ounce can cherry pie filling
    2 tablespoons lemon juice
      Dash ground cloves

Preheat oven to 375°. Meanwhile, shape rolls into eight 6x3½-inch rectangles by sealing perforations between 2 rolls to make one rectangle. Cut meat into ¼-inch cubes; stir in mustard and parsley. Place about ¼ cup meat mixture *on half of each* rectangle; fold unfilled half over to make a turnover. Dampen edges of dough with water; press with fork to seal. Brush tops with milk. Bake on baking sheet at 375° till golden, 15 to 20 minutes.

    Meanwhile, in saucepan combine pie filling, lemon juice, and cloves; heat. Serve over turnovers. Makes 8 turnovers.

Smoky Boys

Heat these sandwiches over a campfire on your next camping adventure—

    1 7-ounce package sliced luncheon
        meat, chopped
    ⅓ cup sliced pimiento-stuffed green
        olives
    ¼ cup chopped celery
    1 cup shredded sharp process
        American cheese (4 ounces)
    ¼ cup catsup
    2 tablespoons fresh or frozen
        chopped onion
    8 hamburger buns, split and toasted

Preheat oven to 400°. Meanwhile, combine first 3 ingredients. Stir in cheese, catsup, and onion. Spread *bottom half of each* bun with about ¼ cup filling; cover with bun top half. Wrap in foil. Heat at 400° for 15 to 20 minutes. Serves 8.

Serve *Reuben Roll-Ups* for lunch or a hearty snack. This flavorful variation of the famous Reuben sandwich is made with sauerkraut, corned beef, and Swiss cheese rolled inside refrigerated roll dough.

Corned Beef Bunwiches

Scoop out part of the hamburger bun centers to make room for the hearty sandwich filling of corned beef, cheese, and pickle —

> 8 hamburger buns, split
> • • •
> 1 12-ounce can corned beef, flaked
> 1 cup shredded sharp process
>   American cheese (4 ounces)
> ½ cup catsup
> ¼ cup coarsely chopped dill pickle
> 1 tablespoon Worcestershire sauce

Preheat oven to 375°. Meanwhile, remove soft centers from hamburger buns. Combine flaked corned beef, shredded sharp process American cheese, catsup, chopped dill pickle, and Worcestershire sauce. Fill buns with corned beef mixture. Wrap each sandwich in foil. Bake at 375° till hot through, about 15 minutes. Serves 8.

Reuben Roll-Ups

> 1 package refrigerated crescent rolls
>   (8 rolls)
> 1 8-ounce can sauerkraut, well drained
>   and snipped
> 1 tablespoon thousand island salad
>   dressing
> 8 thin slices cooked corned beef
>   (about 4 ounces)
> 2 slices process Swiss cheese, cut
>   into 16 strips

Preheat oven to 375°. Separate roll dough into 8 triangles. Mix sauerkraut and dressing. Place one slice meat across wide end of *each* roll triangle. Spread 2 tablespoons sauerkraut mixture on *each* meat slice; top with 2 strips of cheese. Roll up, beginning at wide end. Bake on ungreased baking sheet at 375° till browned, 10 to 15 minutes. Serve hot. Makes 8 roll-ups.

Chili Dogs

Preheat oven to 400°. Meanwhile, make a lengthwise slit in 8 frankfurters; place *each* frankfurter in a buttered frankfurter bun. Open slit. Stir together one 15-ounce can chili with beans and 1 cup crushed corn chips; spoon onto franks in buns. Wrap *each* bun in foil; twist ends to seal. Bake at 400° for 20 minutes. Serve with catsup, if desired. Makes 8 servings.

Tuna and Corn Bake

> 1 cup milk
> 1 beaten egg
> 1 17-ounce can cream-style corn
> 1 9¼-ounce can tuna, drained and
>   flaked
> 1 cup coarse saltine cracker crumbs
> ¼ cup chopped green onion
> ½ teaspoon salt
> 2 tablespoons butter or margarine

Preheat oven to 350°. In saucepan combine milk and egg; add corn. Heat and stir till mixture bubbles. Stir in tuna, *½ cup* coarse cracker crumbs, onion, salt, and dash pepper. Turn into a 1-quart casserole. Melt butter; toss with remaining cracker crumbs. Sprinkle atop casserole. Bake at 350° for 20 minutes. Makes 4 servings.

Oyster Bake

> 1½ pints shucked oysters *or* 2 12-ounce
>   cans frozen oysters, thawed
> ½ of 3½-ounce can French-fried onions
> 2 tablespoons snipped parsley
> 2 tablespoons grated Parmesan cheese
> 2 tablespoons butter or margarine

Preheat oven to 450°. Drain oysters. Sprinkle with salt and pepper. Arrange in buttered 8x1½-inch round baking pan *or* 4 individual baking shells. Cover oysters with onions, parsley, and cheese. Dot with butter. Bake at 450° till browned, 8 to 10 minutes in baking pan and 6 to 8 minutes in individual shells. Serves 4.

Dilled Fish

Preheat oven to 500°. Place two 10-ounce packages frozen, fried, breaded fish portions (8 pieces) in a 15½x10½x1-inch baking pan. Bake fish till heated through, 10 to 12 minutes. Meanwhile, combine ¼ cup dairy sour cream; 2 tablespoons lemon juice; 1 tablespoon dried parsley flakes; 2 teaspoons instant minced onion; and ½ teaspoon dried dillweed, crushed. To serve, spoon sour cream mixture over fish. Serves 4.

Egg-Rice Bake

> ¾ cup uncooked packaged precooked
>   rice
> ¾ cup milk
> 3 tablespoons finely chopped green
>   onion
> 3 tablespoons snipped parsley
> 1 beaten egg
> ¼ teaspoon salt
> 6 eggs

Preheat oven to 350°. Meanwhile, cook rice according to package directions. Combine milk, green onion, parsley, 1 beaten egg, and salt. Add to rice; mix well. Spoon into six 5-ounce custard cups. Break *1 egg into each* custard cup. Sprinkle with salt. Bake at 350° till eggs are done and rice is set, 20 to 25 minutes. Serves 6.

Ham-Bean Bake
Accomplish other tasks while this bakes —

> 2 cups cubed fully cooked ham
> 2 16-ounce cans pork and beans in
>   tomato sauce
> 2 tablespoons molasses
> 2 tablespoons catsup
> 2 teaspoons instant minced onion
> 2 teaspoons Worcestershire sauce
> 1 teaspoon prepared mustard

Preheat oven to 375°. In mixing bowl combine all ingredients. Spoon into 6 individual casseroles. Bake, uncovered, at 375° till heated through, 25 to 30 minutes. Serves 6.

Out of the Skillet

Steak de Burgo

An elegant entrée for two—

2 tablespoons butter
1 clove garlic, minced
1 teaspoon dried basil,
    crushed
2 4-ounce beef tenderloin slices
2 large fresh mushrooms, fluted
2 slices French bread, toasted

In heavy skillet melt butter, Stir in garlic and basil. Sprinkle meat with salt and freshly ground pepper; add to skillet along with mushrooms. Panbroil the meat over medium-high heat. Allow 4 minutes on each side for rare and 6 to 7 minutes on each side for medium. Serve tenderloin atop bread; pour pan drippings over. Top with mushroom. Makes 2 servings.

Chicken Curry

4 slices bacon
¼ cup sliced celery
¼ cup fresh or frozen chopped onion
1 clove garlic, minced
2 tablespoons all-purpose flour
1 cup milk
½ cup applesauce
3 tablespoons tomato paste
3 to 4 teaspoons curry powder
2 chicken bouillon cubes
3 cups cubed cooked chicken
    Hot cooked rice
    Toasted coconut or chutney

Cook bacon till crisp; drain and crumble, reserving 1 tablespoon drippings. Cook celery, onion, and garlic in reserved drippings; blend in flour. Add milk, applesauce, tomato paste, curry, bouillon cubes, and 1 cup water. Cook and stir till thick. Stir in chicken and crumbled bacon; heat through. Serve over rice. Pass coconut or chutney. Serves 6 to 8.

Egg-Stuffed Zucchini

Prepare this brunch entrée in two skillets. Simmer squash halves in one while you scramble the egg mixture in the other—

4 medium zucchini (1½ pounds)
½ cup water
    Salt
1 tomato, chopped (1 cup)
2 tablespoons butter or
    margarine
3 beaten eggs
¼ teaspoon salt
    Dash pepper
          • • •
½ cup shredded sharp process
    American cheese (2 ounces)

Wash zucchini; halve lengthwise but do not peel. Scoop out pulp, leaving ¼-inch shell. Chop pulp from zucchini to make 1 cup; set chopped zucchini aside.

Place the zucchini shells, cut side down, in large skillet. Add ½ cup water and simmer, covered, till zucchini is just tender, 5 to 6 minutes. Drain and turn cut side up in same skillet. Season shells with a little salt. Meanwhile, in medium skillet cook the zucchini pulp and chopped tomato in butter till zucchini is tender, about 3 minutes. Add eggs, ¼ teaspoon salt, and pepper to zucchini-tomato mixture; cook over low heat till just set, lifting with a spatula so uncooked portion can run underneath. Spoon scrambled egg mixture into zucchini shells. Top with shredded sharp process American cheese. Heat, covered, just till cheese melts, about 2 minutes. Makes 4 servings.

Fresh from the garden or market

Choose fresh zucchini, tomato, and eggs with care for elegant *Egg Stuffed Zucchini*. This tasty skillet dish is a perfect choice for the entrée of a special brunch, luncheon, or supper.

Chinese Pork and Vegetables

½ cup cold water
¼ cup soy sauce
1 tablespoon cornstarch
2 tablespoons cooking oil
1 clove garlic, minced
1 teaspoon grated gingerroot
    Dash salt
1 pound lean pork, diced
3 cups chopped Chinese or celery
    cabbage
1 10-ounce package frozen peas,
    thawed
1 medium green pepper, cut in thin
    strips
1 3-ounce can sliced mushrooms,
    drained
2 tablespoons sliced green
    onion
2 tablespoons dry sherry
    Hot cooked rice

Combine water, soy sauce, and cornstarch; set aside. Heat wok on range till hot. Add oil; reduce heat to medium. Add garlic, gingerroot, and salt; stir-fry till garlic is golden. Turn heat to high; add pork gradually, stirring mixture constantly till browned, 2 to 4 minutes. Season with additional salt. Add cabbage, peas, green pepper, mushrooms, onion, and sherry. Cook and stir 1 minute more. Pour soy mixture over vegetables; cook and stir till thickened. Serve with rice. Makes 4 servings.

Mexican-Style Eggs

Tear 6 canned or frozen tortillas in bite-sized pieces. In skillet fry tortillas in 2 tablespoons butter. Push tortillas to edge of skillet, making a well. Add 3 beaten eggs; cook and stir till softly scrambled. Mix in ½ pound ground beef and one 10-ounce can enchilada sauce.

Sprinkle ½ cup sliced green onion and ½ cup sliced ripe olives over. Cook, covered, for 10 to 15 minutes. Stir in ½ cup dairy sour cream and ½ cup shredded process American cheese (2 ounces). Cook till heated through, *but do not boil.* Serves 4.

Speedy Beef Stroganoff

Cut the meat while it's partially frozen —

1 pound beef sirloin steak, cut
    ¼ inch thick, partially frozen
1 tablespoon all-purpose flour
1 3-ounce can sliced mushrooms
½ cup boiling water
1 teaspoon instant beef bouillon
    granules
1 cup onion-sour cream dip
    Hot cooked noodles

Trim fat from steak; cook trimmings in skillet till 1 tablespoon of fat accumulates. Discard trimmings. Meanwhile, cut meat diagonally across grain in very thin strips. Quickly brown meat. Blend in flour. Add undrained mushrooms, water, and beef bouillon granules. Cook and stir till thickened and bubbly. Simmer 10 minutes. Blend some of the meat mixture into sour cream dip. Return to meat mixture. Cook and stir till heated through, *but do not boil.* Serve over noodles. Makes 4 or 5 servings.

Quick Spanish Rice

Canned meat makes it fast to prepare —

½ cup fresh or frozen chopped green
    pepper
½ cup fresh or frozen chopped onion
¼ cup water
    • • •
2 cups uncooked packaged
    precooked rice
2 cups water
1 8-ounce can tomato sauce
2 tablespoons chili sauce
1 teaspoon sugar
    Dash pepper
1 12-ounce can luncheon meat, cut
    in thin strips

In 10-inch skillet cook green pepper and onion in ¼ cup water till tender, 2 to 3 minutes. Stir in rice, 2 cups water, tomato sauce, chili sauce, sugar, and pepper. Stir in meat. Bring to boil; reduce heat. Cover; cook over low heat till rice is tender, about 10 minutes. Makes 4 to 6 servings.

Chicken Liver Stroganoff

A fancy liver and onion entrée —

      1 medium onion, sliced
      2 tablespoons butter or margarine
      2 8-ounce packages frozen chicken
          livers, thawed
      1 3-ounce can sliced mushrooms
      2 teaspoons paprika
      ½ teaspoon salt
          Dash pepper
               •   •   •
      1 tablespoon all-purpose flour
      1 cup dairy sour cream
          Hot cooked rice

Cook onion in butter or margarine till tender but not brown. Halve each chicken liver; add to onion mixture with undrained mushrooms. Stir in paprika, salt, and pepper. Cover; cook over low heat till livers are tender, 8 to 10 minutes, stirring frequently. Stir the all-purpose flour into the dairy sour cream; stir into the liver mixture. Heat the mixture through, *but do not boil*. Serve over hot cooked rice. Makes 6 servings.

Steak Skillet Supper

Meat and vegetable dish in one —

      1 pound beef round steak, cut into
          thin strips
      1 tablespoon cooking oil
      1 10½-ounce can mushroom gravy
      ½ cup water
      ½ envelope spaghetti sauce mix with
          mushrooms (about 2 tablespoons)
               •   •   •
      3 to 4 medium zucchini, cut in
          1½-inch slices
          Hot cooked noodles or rice

In skillet quickly brown the round steak strips in hot cooking oil. Add mushroom gravy, water, and spaghetti sauce mix; stir till well combined. Cover; cook over low heat for 20 minutes, stirring occasionally. Add zucchini slices. Cover and continue cooking till zucchini is crisp-tender, 10 to 12 minutes. Serve zucchini mixture over hot noodles or rice. Serves 4.

Turkey Jambalaya

Frozen turkey and gravy shortcut this dish —

      ¾ cup long grain rice
      ½ cup chopped celery
      ¼ cup fresh or frozen chopped green
          pepper
      ¼ cup fresh or frozen chopped onion
      ¼ cup butter or margarine
               •   •   •
      1 16-ounce can tomatoes, cut up
      ¼ teaspoon dried thyme, crushed
          Dash cayenne
      1 28-ounce package frozen, sliced
          turkey and giblet gravy

In large skillet cook rice, celery, green pepper, and onion in butter or margarine till vegetables are tender and rice is browned, stirring occasionally.

Meanwhile, mix tomatoes, crushed thyme, and cayenne; stir into rice mixture. Place frozen block of sliced turkey atop rice mixture. Cover and simmer till turkey is hot and rice is tender, about 30 minutes, stirring occasionally. Remove from heat; let stand 5 minutes before serving. Serves 5 or 6.

Steak Skillet Supper will win approval from the whole family. Enjoy this hearty steak-zucchini combination served over hot noodles or rice.

Swiss Veal in Cream

½ cup fresh or frozen chopped onion
1 clove garlic, minced
¼ cup butter or margarine
6 veal cutlets, cut ½ inch thick
1 cup whipping cream
½ pound fresh mushrooms
2 tablespoons butter or
    margarine
3 to 4 tablespoons cognac *or*
    brandy
Hot cooked noodles

In 10- or 12-inch skillet cook onion and garlic in ¼ cup butter till onion is tender but not brown; add veal and cook till it loses its pink color, about 6 to 7 minutes. Season with 1 teaspoon salt and dash pepper; add cream and simmer, covered, 10 minutes more.

Meanwhile, slice mushrooms; cook in 2 tablespoons butter about 2 to 3 minutes. Add mushrooms and cognac or brandy to veal. Serve with hot noodles. Serves 6.

Saucy Lamb Chops

4 lamb shoulder chops
2 tablespoons cooking oil
¾ cup water
½ cup chopped celery
⅓ cup sliced green onion with tops
1 teaspoon instant beef bouillon
    granules
¼ teaspoon dried thyme, crushed
1 3-ounce can chopped mushrooms
2 tablespoons all-purpose flour
1 tablespoon snipped parsley
Hot cooked rice

In large skillet brown the chops on both sides in hot oil; sprinkle with salt and pepper. Drain off excess fat; add water, celery, green onion, bouillon granules, and thyme. Cover; simmer 20 minutes. Remove chops to platter; keep warm. Drain mushrooms, reserving liquid; mix liquid and flour. Stir into cooking liquid; cook, stirring constantly, till thickened and bubbly. Add chopped mushrooms and snipped parsley. Serve sauce over rice. Makes 4 servings.

Veal Epicurean

Dry white wine adds a gourmet touch—

1 tablespoon cooking oil
1 tablespoon butter or margarine
2 pounds veal round steak, cut in
    thin strips
3 tablespoons all-purpose flour
¾ teaspoon salt
⅛ teaspoon pepper
1½ cups water
1 chicken bouillon cube
• • •
½ pound small onions, cut in
    eighths (about 2 cups)
½ cup dry white wine
2 tablespoons snipped parsley
1 bay leaf
Hot cooked rice

In large skillet heat together oil and butter or margarine. Add veal, a small amount at a time, and brown lightly. Push meat to one side; blend flour, salt, and pepper into drippings in skillet. Add water and bouillon cube; cook and stir till mixture boils. Stir with veal. Reduce heat; stir in onions, wine, parsley, and bay leaf. Cover and simmer till the veal and the onions are tender, about 25 minutes, stirring the mixture occasionally. Remove the bay leaf; serve over hot cooked rice. Makes 6 servings.

Ham with Orange Sauce

Bits of shredded orange peel perk up this unusual orange and cream sauce—

Trim excess fat from one 1½-pound fully cooked ham slice, cut ¾ inch thick; slash remaining fat edge of ham. Cook trimmings in skillet till 1 tablespoon fat accumulates. Discard trimmings and brown the ham slowly on both sides in hot fat. Remove ham to warm platter and keep warm.

Shred 1 teaspoon orange peel; set aside. Mix ½ cup orange juice and 1 teaspoon cornstarch; add to skillet. Cook and stir till bubbly. Add ¾ cup light cream, ⅛ teaspoon salt, and reserved peel; cook and stir till thickened, 2 to 3 minutes. Serve sauce with ham. Makes 6 servings.

Fish in Beer Batter

If possible, use freshly caught fish—

Beat together 1¼ cups packaged biscuit mix, ¾ cup beer, 1 egg, and ¼ teaspoon salt. Pat 4 pan-dressed fish (about 8 ounces each) with paper toweling to dry. Coat fish with batter. In skillet fry the fish in hot cooking oil till they are done, 4 to 5 minutes on *each* side. Makes 4 servings.

Sautéed Liver

Lemon juice and Worcestershire add flavor—

Cook 1 cup sliced onion in 2 tablespoons butter, margarine, *or* bacon drippings till tender but not brown. Remove from skillet.

Add 4 slices beef liver, cut ⅜ inch thick (about 1 pound); sprinkle with salt and pepper. Cook 3 minutes at medium heat; turn. Return onions to skillet; cook 3 minutes more. Remove liver and onions.

Add 2 teaspoons lemon juice and 1 teaspoon Worcestershire sauce to skillet, stirring to blend with drippings. Pour over liver. Makes 4 servings.

Beef in Wine Sauce

This dish is both delicious and attractive—

 4 slices French bread, diagonally
 sliced
 ¼ cup butter or margarine, softened
 4 beef boneless strip steaks, cut
 ½ inch thick (about 1½ pounds)
 2 tablespoons butter or
 margarine
 ¼ cup port
 ½ cup whipping cream

Spread bread on both sides with the ¼ cup butter. In skillet toast bread until golden brown. Remove to plates. Brown the steaks on both sides in 2 tablespoons butter. Allow about 10 minutes for medium-rare. Season with salt and pepper. Place steaks atop bread. Add port to skillet; stir to blend with drippings. Add cream; cook and stir till thickened and bubbly. Season with salt. Pour over meat. Serves 4.

Meatball Dinner

 1 10-ounce package frozen limas
 1 pound ground beef
 ½ teaspoon salt
 ¼ cup fresh or frozen chopped onion
 Cooking oil
 1 10½-ounce can condensed beef
 broth
 1 soup can water (1⅓ cups)
 1 cup sliced celery
 1 cup sliced carrots
 ¼ cup cold water
 2½ tablespoons cornstarch
 1 tablespoon soy sauce
 Hot cooked rice

Cook limas according to package directions. Meanwhile, mix beef and salt; shape into 20 meatballs. Brown with onion in a little hot oil; drain. Stir in beef broth, 1⅓ cups water, celery, carrots, and cooked limas. Cover and cook 15 minutes. Blend ¼ cup cold water, cornstarch, and soy sauce; add to skillet. Cook and stir till thickened and bubbly. Serve with rice. Makes 5 servings.

Chow Mein Burgers

 1 pound ground beef
 ½ cup fresh or frozen chopped onion
 1 16-ounce can chop suey vegetables,
 drained
 ⅓ cup cold water
 3 tablespoons soy sauce
 2 tablespoons cornstarch
 8 hamburger buns, split, toasted,
 and buttered
 1 3-ounce can chow mein noodles

In medium skillet combine ground beef and chopped onion; cook till meat is lightly browned and onion is tender. Add chop suey vegetables. Stir water and soy sauce into cornstarch; stir into beef mixture and cook 1 to 2 minutes, stirring to coat vegetables and meat. Spoon mixture onto bottom halves of toasted hamburger buns. Crumble a few chow mein noodles over each sandwich; cover with top halves of hamburger buns. Makes 8 servings.

From the Saucepan

Scallop Creole

½ cup fresh or frozen chopped onion
½ cup fresh or frozen chopped green
    pepper
1 clove garlic, minced
2 tablespoons cooking oil
1 16-ounce can tomatoes, cut up
1 8-ounce can tomato sauce
1 teaspoon sugar
¼ teaspoon dried thyme, crushed
¼ teaspoon dried basil, crushed
2 bay leaves
1 pound fresh scallops *or* frozen
    scallops, thawed
2 tablespoons cornstarch
Hot cooked rice

Cook onion, green pepper, and garlic in oil till tender. Add next 6 ingredients, ½ teaspoon salt, and ⅛ teaspoon pepper. Cover; simmer 15 minutes. Meanwhile, cut scallops in ¾-inch pieces; add to tomato mixture and simmer 5 minutes. Remove bay leaves. Blend cornstarch and ¼ cup cold water; add to mixture. Cook and stir till thickened. Serve over rice. Serves 4.

Lazy-Day Lobster Newburg

1⅓ cups light cream
1 envelope white sauce mix (enough
    for 1 cup sauce)
2 beaten egg yolks
1 5-ounce can lobster,
    drained and flaked
2 tablespoons dry sherry
Toast points
Paprika

Slowly stir cream into sauce mix; cook and stir till bubbly. Stir some of hot mixture into yolks; return to remaining hot mixture. Cook and stir till bubbly. Add lobster and sherry; heat through. Serve over toast; dash with paprika. Serves 4.

Chicken Aloha

1½ cups sliced celery
1 green pepper, cut in strips
3 tablespoons butter or margarine
3 cups cubed cooked chicken
1 22-ounce can pineapple pie filling
¼ cup soy sauce
2 teaspoons instant chicken bouillon
    granules
Chow mein noodles
Slivered almonds and coconut

Cook vegetables in butter till crisp-tender. Add next 4 ingredients and ⅓ cup water; cook and stir till hot. Serve over noodles. Pass nuts and coconut. Serves 6.

Wine-Sauced Chicken

3 whole large chicken breasts,
    halved, skinned, and boned
⅓ cup dry sherry
¼ cup butter or margarine
1 cup sliced fresh mushrooms
½ cup light cream
2 egg yolks
Paprika

Cook chicken, covered, in sherry and butter over medium heat till tender, about 25 minutes. Add mushrooms; cook 3 minutes. Remove chicken to warm platter. Beat cream, yolks, and ¼ teaspoon salt just till blended; add to cooking liquid. Cook and stir till thickened. Serve over chicken; sprinkle with paprika. Makes 4 servings.

Saucy chicken dish

Combine chicken with pineapple pie filling and green pepper strips to create delectable *Chicken Aloha*. Garnish with parsley sprigs and kumquats, and pass almonds and coconut. →

Pork and Rice Supper

Use a pressure cooker for this main dish —

2 teaspoons shortening
4 pork chops, cut ¾ inch thick
1 6-ounce package long grain and
    wild rice mix
1 3-ounce can sliced mushrooms
1 13¾-ounce can chicken broth
1 tablespoon instant minced onion
    Snipped parsley

Heat shortening in 4-quart pressure cooker. Trim fat off pork chops. Brown the chops in hot shortening; sprinkle with salt and pepper. Combine long grain and wild rice mix and undrained sliced mushrooms; spoon rice mixture over chops. Combine chicken broth and instant minced onion; pour over chops and rice. Close cover of pressure cooker securely. Put pressure regulator in place; cook 15 to 17 minutes with pressure regulator rocking *very gently* (15 pounds pressure). Reduce pressure quickly under cold running water. Remove cover. Garnish pork chops and rice with snipped parsley. Makes 4 servings.

Frank and Bean Combo

1 16-ounce can kidney beans, drained
1 16-ounce can butter beans
1 16-ounce can pork and beans in
    tomato sauce
½ cup catsup
¼ cup packed brown sugar
1 tablespoon instant minced onion
1 teaspoon dry mustard
½ teaspoon Worcestershire sauce
⅛ teaspoon garlic powder

• • •

½ pound frankfurters, cut in 1-inch
    pieces

In saucepan combine kidney beans, undrained butter beans, pork and beans in tomato sauce, catsup, brown sugar, instant minced onion, dry mustard, Worcestershire sauce, and garlic powder. Simmer, uncovered, for 10 minutes. Add frankfurter pieces and heat through. Makes 6 servings.

Sweet-Sour Tuna

1 10½-ounce can chicken gravy
¼ cup sugar
2 tablespoons vinegar
2 tablespoons soy sauce
1 medium green pepper, cut in
    ¾-inch squares
1 13½-ounce can pineapple tidbits,
    drained
1 9¼-ounce can tuna, drained and
    broken into chunks
    Hot cooked rice *or* 1 3-ounce can
    chow mein noodles

In medium saucepan combine chicken gravy, sugar, vinegar, and soy sauce; add green pepper squares. Bring gravy mixture to boiling; cover and simmer 8 minutes, stirring occasionally. Add drained pineapple tidbits and tuna chunks. Cook mixture till tuna and pineapple are heated through, about 2 minutes more. Serve tuna-pineapple mixture over hot cooked rice or chow mein noodles. Makes 4 servings.

Ham Bunwiches

½ cup fresh or frozen chopped green
    pepper
½ cup fresh or frozen chopped onion
2 tablespoons cooking oil
1 8-ounce can kidney beans,
    drained (1 cup)
1 8-ounce can tomato sauce
1 teaspoon chili powder
1 12-ounce can chopped ham, cut in
    strips
½ cup shredded process American
    cheese (2 ounces)
8 to 10 frankfurter buns, split
    and toasted

In medium saucepan cook green pepper and onion in hot oil till tender but not brown. Stir in kidney beans, tomato sauce, and chili powder; mix well. Add ham and shredded process American cheese; cook and stir till cheese melts and mixture is heated through. Spoon ham-bean mixture into toasted buns. Makes 8 to 10 servings.

Shrimp-Filled Tortillas

This unique dish is shown on page 2—

Cooking oil
1 7-ounce can frozen
avocado dip, thawed
1 cup dairy sour cream
Dash bottled hot pepper sauce
1 tablespoon snipped parsley
¼ teaspoon onion powder
2 4½-ounce cans shrimp, drained
12 canned tortillas *or* frozen
tortillas, thawed

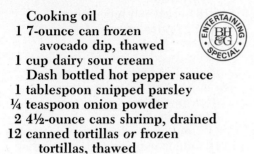

Preheat oven to 300°. Pour cooking oil into deep saucepan to depth of 2 inches; heat atop range to 350°. Meanwhile, mix dip, ¼ *cup* of the sour cream, and hot pepper sauce; set aside. Combine remaining sour cream, parsley, and onion powder; fold in shrimp. Place 3 or 4 tortillas at a time on baking sheet. Soften in oven for 1 minute. *Quickly* place a generous 2 tablespoons shrimp mixture on *each* soft tortilla. Roll up tightly; secure with wooden pick. Carefully fry 3 or 4 filled tortillas at a time in the deep hot fat (350°) till tortillas are crisp, 1 to 2 minutes. Carefully remove and drain. Keep the tortillas warm in the oven. Repeat with remaining tortillas. Spoon avocado mixture over. Makes 4 to 6 servings.

Hearty German Supper

1 16-ounce can applesauce (2 cups)
1 14-ounce can sauerkraut, drained
and snipped
⅓ cup dry white wine
2 tablespoons packed brown sugar
12-ounces Polish sausage
1 16-ounce can whole onions, drained
1 16-ounce can whole new potatoes,
drained

In large saucepan combine first 4 ingredients. Add remaining ingredients. Simmer, uncovered, about 20 minutes, stirring occasionally. Arrange sauerkraut mixture on platter with onions and potatoes in ring around sausage. Garnish with snipped parsley, if desired. Makes 4 servings.

Chili over Rice

1 pound ground beef
1 tablespoon instant minced onion
1 16-ounce can kidney beans
1 10¾-ounce can condensed tomato
soup
1 to 2 teaspoons chili powder
½ teaspoon salt
½ teaspoon dried oregano, crushed
⅛ teaspoon pepper
Hot cooked rice

In large saucepan cook beef and onion till beef is browned. Stir in undrained kidney beans, soup, chili powder, salt, oregano, and pepper; heat through. Serve over hot cooked rice. Makes 4 servings.

Corned Beef Barbecue

Cook ¼ cup fresh or frozen chopped onion and 2 tablespoons fresh or frozen chopped green pepper in 2 tablespoons hot cooking oil till tender. Stir in one 12-ounce can corned beef, flaked, and ¾ cup chili sauce. Cook, stirring occasionally, till heated through. Serve in 6 to 8 hamburger buns, split and toasted. Serves 6 to 8.

Saucy Frank and Noodle Supper

6 frankfurters
4 ounces uncooked medium noodles
(about 3 cups)
1 28-ounce can tomatoes, cut up
1 cup chopped celery
1 1½-ounce envelope spaghetti
sauce mix
1 teaspoon sugar
½ cup shredded sharp process
American cheese (2 ounces)

Cut franks diagonally in thirds; place in large saucepan. Add noodles, tomatoes, celery, spaghetti sauce mix, sugar, and ½ cup water. Stir to moisten noodles. Cover; cook over low heat, stirring often, till noodles are done, about 15 minutes. Sprinkle with cheese. Makes 6 servings.

Quick Spaghetti Sauce

1 pound ground beef
½ pound Italian sausage
1 15-ounce can tomato sauce
1 6-ounce can tomato paste
1 cup fresh or frozen chopped onion
½ cup dry red wine *or* water
1 3-ounce can sliced mushrooms
1 teaspoon dried oregano, crushed
½ teaspoon garlic powder
   Hot cooked spaghetti
   Grated Parmesan cheese

In 4-quart pressure cooker brown the beef and sausage; drain off fat. Add tomato sauce and paste, onion, wine, undrained mushrooms, oregano, and garlic powder. Close cover securely. Put pressure regulator in place; cook 10 minutes with pressure regulator rocking slowly (15 pounds pressure). Reduce pressure quickly under cold running water. Remove cover. Serve over spaghetti. Pass cheese. Serves 6 to 8.

Ravioli Soup

3 cups water
1 18-ounce can tomato juice
1 10½-ounce can condensed
   beef broth
1 cup diced carrots (2 medium)
1 cup diced potato (1 medium)
¼ cup sliced green onion
1 teaspoon sugar
1 teaspoon salt
1 15-ounce can beef ravioli in sauce
1 8-ounce can spinach, drained
   and snipped

In large saucepan or Dutch oven combine water, tomato juice, condensed beef broth, diced carrots, diced potato, sliced green onion, sugar, and salt. Bring tomato mixture to boiling. Reduce heat; cover and simmer till vegetables are tender, 12 to 15 minutes. Gently stir in beef ravioli in sauce and snipped spinach. Heat through. Serve in soup bowls. Makes 8 servings.

Cooked ham, sharp American cheese, and vegetables give *Ham-Cheese Chowder* its full-bodied flavor. Serve everyone generous portions of this thick and creamy soup and watch them react with delight.

Ham-Cheese Chowder

½ cup coarsely shredded carrot
¼ cup fresh or frozen chopped onion
¼ cup butter or margarine
3 tablespoons all-purpose flour
4 cups milk
1½ cups diced fully cooked ham
½ teaspoon celery seed
½ teaspoon Worcestershire sauce
1 cup sharp process American
    cheese, cut in cubes (4 ounces)
Snipped chives (optional)

In large saucepan cook carrot and onion in butter till tender but not brown. Blend in flour; add milk. Cook and stir till thickened and bubbly. Stir in diced ham, celery seed, and Worcestershire; heat through. Add process American cheese; stir till melted. Garnish with snipped chives, if desired. Makes 4 or 5 servings.

Chicken and Noodles

This tasty dish cooks in a pressure cooker—

1 2½- to 3-pound ready-to-cook
    broiler-fryer chicken, cut up
3 cups water
1 carrot, peeled and sliced
1 tablespoon instant minced onion
1 teaspoon salt
½ teaspoon celery salt
⅛ teaspoon pepper
3 cups medium noodles
1 tablespoon dried parsley flakes
½ teaspoon dried basil, crushed

Remove excess fat from chicken. In 4-quart pressure cooker combine chicken, *1 cup* of the water, sliced carrot, instant minced onion, salt, celery salt, and pepper. Close cover securely. Put pressure regulator in place; cook 10 minutes with pressure regulator rocking slowly (15 pounds pressure). Reduce pressure quickly under cold running water. Remove cover. Add noodles, remaining water, dried parsley flakes, and crushed basil; cover *but do not seal.* Cook over medium heat till noodles are done, about 10 minutes. Makes 6 servings.

Corned Beef Stew

Serve this hearty main dish stew piping hot—

2 11-ounce cans condensed split pea
    soup
1 soup can water (1⅓ cups)
1 12-ounce can corned beef, cubed
1 8-ounce can mixed vegetables
1 cup packaged biscuit mix

In saucepan combine soup, the soup can of water, corned beef, and undrained mixed vegetables. Bring mixture to boiling. Stir together biscuit mix and ⅓ cup water; spoon dough onto boiling stew. Cook, uncovered, for 10 minutes. Cover and cook 10 minutes more. Stir soup mixture before serving. Makes 4 to 6 servings.

Smoky Corn Chowder

½ cup fresh or frozen chopped onion
¼ cup butter or margarine
¼ cup all-purpose flour
4 cups milk
1 16-ounce can whole kernel corn,
    drained
1 12-ounce package smoked sausage
    links, sliced (8 links)
1 8-ounce can limas, drained

Cook onion in butter till tender but not brown. Blend in flour, 1 teaspoon salt, and ⅛ teaspoon pepper. Add milk all at once. Cook and stir till thickened and bubbly. Stir in corn, sausage, and limas; simmer 10 minutes. Makes 6 servings.

Sour Cream Chili

In large saucepan brown 1 pound ground beef; drain. Add two 11-ounce cans condensed chili beef soup, 2 cups water, 2 tablespoons dry onion soup mix, and 1 to 1½ teaspoons chili powder. Bring to boiling; cover and simmer 5 minutes. Stir some of hot mixture into 1 cup dairy sour cream; return to remaining hot mixture. Heat through *but do not boil.* Garnish with grated cheese and chopped onion. Serves 6.

Under the Broiler

Chutney Grilled Lamb Chops

½ cup chutney, finely chopped
2 tablespoons butter or
    margarine, melted
1 tablespoon lemon juice
1 teaspoon curry powder
4 lamb loin chops, cut ¾ inch thick

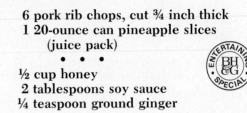

Preheat broiler. Combine all ingredients *except* lamb chops. Place chops on rack in broiler pan; brush with *half* the chutney mixture. Broil 3 to 4 inches from heat for 10 minutes. Turn chops; brush with remaining chutney mixture. Broil 8 to 10 minutes more. Makes 4 servings.

Thyme-Topped Fish

2 12-ounce packages frozen halibut
    steaks, thawed
6 tablespoons butter, melted
½ cup fine dry bread crumbs
¼ teaspoon dried thyme, crushed
⅛ teaspoon garlic salt

Preheat broiler. Place fish on rack in broiler pan; brush with *some* of the butter. Season with salt and pepper. Broil 4 inches from heat for 5 minutes. Turn; brush again with butter. Season with salt and pepper; broil 3 minutes. Combine remaining butter and last 3 ingredients; sprinkle on fish. Broil 3 to 5 minutes. Serves 6.

Peanut Butter Burgers

Preheat broiler. Combine 2 slightly beaten eggs, 2 pounds ground beef, ½ cup fresh or frozen chopped onion, ¼ cup chunk-style peanut butter, 1 teaspoon salt, and ¼ teaspoon pepper. Shape into 8 patties. Broil on broiler pan for 6 to 7 minutes. Top with dill pickle slices; serve in 8 hamburger buns, split and toasted. Serves 8.

Polynesian-Style Chops

6 pork rib chops, cut ¾ inch thick
1 20-ounce can pineapple slices
    (juice pack)
• • •
½ cup honey
2 tablespoons soy sauce
¼ teaspoon ground ginger

Preheat broiler. Place pork chops on broiler pan; broil 4 to 5 inches from heat for 8 minutes. Turn chops; broil 6 minutes more. Meanwhile, drain pineapple slices, reserving 2 tablespoons juice. Combine honey, reserved juice, soy sauce, and ginger. Place one slice pineapple atop *each* chop; broil 5 to 8 minutes more, basting frequently with honey-ginger mixture. Spoon remaining honey mixture over pork chops before serving. Makes 6 servings.

Fish Kabobs

Preheat broiler. Cut 2 green peppers and 2 pounds frozen codfish or halibut, thawed, into 1½-inch pieces. Combine 3 tablespoons lemon juice, 3 tablespoons cooking oil, ½ to 1 teaspoon Italian seasoning, ¼ teaspoon salt, ¼ teaspoon paprika, and dash pepper. Brush on fish; sprinkle lightly with salt. On 4 skewers alternately thread fish and green pepper pieces. Brush with oil mixture. Broil 4 to 6 inches from heat for 8 to 10 minutes, turning once and brushing with additional oil mixture. Serve with lemon wedges. Makes 6 servings.

Elegant company entrée

Prepare *Polynesian-Style Chops* the next time →
you entertain guests. As these pineapple-topped pork chops cook under the broiler, baste them with a flavorful honey-ginger sauce.

Marinated Beef Broil

½ cup pineapple juice
1 envelope all-purpose meat
     marinade mix
2 tablespoons lemon juice
¼ teaspoon dried basil, crushed
1 clove garlic, minced
• • •
2 pounds beef round steak, cut
     1 inch thick

Preheat broiler. Gradually stir pineapple juice into marinade mix. Add lemon juice, basil, and garlic. Place meat in shallow pan; pour marinade over. Pierce all surfaces of meat deeply with fork. Let stand 15 minutes, turning meat several times. Drain, reserving marinade. Place meat on rack in broiler pan. Broil 3 inches from heat for 10 minutes. Turn; brush with *some* of the marinade. Broil till meat is of desired doneness. Meanwhile, stir ½ cup water into reserved marinade. Heat to boiling. Reduce heat; simmer 5 minutes. Pass with steak. Makes 6 servings.

Bologna Kabobs

1 13½-ounce can pineapple chunks,
     drained
2 green peppers, cut in 1-inch
     pieces
8 ounces unsliced bologna, cut in
     1 x 1 x ½-inch pieces
• • •
½ cup hot-style catsup
2 tablespoons finely chopped onion
2 tablespoons cooking oil
1 tablespoon lemon juice
1 teaspoon dry mustard
8 frankfurter buns, split and toasted

Preheat broiler. Alternately thread 8 skewers with pineapple, green pepper, and bologna pieces. For sauce, combine hot-style catsup, onion, cooking oil, lemon juice, and dry mustard. Broil kabobs 3 to 4 inches from heat for 8 to 10 minutes, brushing frequently with sauce. Turn kabobs often. Serve kabobs on toasted frankfurter buns. Pass remaining sauce. Makes 8 sandwiches.

Ham with Peanut Butter Glaze

1 fully cooked ham center cut slice,
     cut ½ inch thick (about 1 pound)
3 tablespoons orange marmalade
2 tablespoons peanut butter
1 tablespoon water

Preheat broiler. Slash edges of ham slice; place on broiler pan. Broil 3 inches from heat for 5 minutes. Turn ham; broil 4 to 5 minutes more. Meanwhile, combine marmalade, peanut butter, and water. Spoon atop ham slice. Broil till lightly browned, ½ to 1 minute more. Makes 4 servings.

Corned Beef Hash Burgers

Preheat broiler. Split and toast 8 onion rolls. Combine one 15-ounce can corned beef hash, ⅓ cup dairy sour cream, 1 tablespoon pickle relish, and 1 teaspoon prepared horseradish. Spread about ¼ cup mixture on bottom half of *each* roll. Broil 3 to 4 inches from heat till hot, about 5 minutes. Top *each* with one slice tomato and one slice process American cheese; broil just till cheese melts. Cover with roll tops. Makes 8 sandwiches.

Ground Beef Logs

¼ cup finely crushed cornflakes
¼ cup dairy sour cream
1 slightly beaten egg
2 tablespoons chopped ripe olives
2 tablespoons chili sauce
1 tablespoon snipped parsley
½ teaspoon instant minced onion
1 pound ground beef
6 frankfurter buns, split and toasted

Preheat broiler. In mixing bowl combine cornflakes, sour cream, egg, chopped ripe olives, chili sauce, parsley, instant minced onion, ½ teaspoon salt, and dash pepper. Add ground beef; mix well. Shape into 6 logs to fit buns. Broil on broiler pan 3 inches from heat till done, 9 to 10 minutes, turning occasionally. Serve beef logs in toasted frankfurter buns. Makes 6 sandwiches.

Hawaiian Windups

Wrap ham strips around frankfurters and pineapple spears for a tasty broiler sandwich—

    1 15¼-ounce can pineapple spears
    3 tablespoons packed brown sugar
    1 tablespoon cornstarch
    ¼ cup vinegar
    ¼ cup butter or margarine
         • • •
    8 frankfurter buns, split and toasted
    8 frankfurters or smoked sausage
      links
    4 slices boiled ham

Preheat broiler. Drain pineapple spears, reserving ½ cup syrup. In saucepan combine brown sugar and cornstarch. Stir in reserved syrup, vinegar, and butter. Cook, stirring constantly, till thickened and bubbly. Brush inside of each bun with sauce. Slit frankfurters or sausage links lengthwise; place 1½ pineapple spears in *each* slit. Cut *each* ham slice into 4 strips. Wrap *each* frankfurter or sausage link with two ham strips; secure with wooden picks. Broil 3 to 4 inches from heat till frankfurters or sausage links are heated through, about 5 minutes, basting occasionally with sauce. Serve in buns. Pass remaining sauce. Makes 8 sandwiches.

Tangy Kraut Burgers

    1½ pounds ground beef
    1 8-ounce can sauerkraut, drained
      and snipped
    ¼ cup Italian salad dressing
    1 tablespoon instant minced onion
    ½ teaspoon caraway seed
    ¼ teaspoon salt
    6 hamburger buns, split and toasted

Preheat broiler. Combine ground beef, sauerkraut, Italian dressing, instant minced onion, caraway seed, and salt. Shape into 6 patties, ¾ inch thick. Broil on broiler pan 3 inches from heat for 6 minutes. Turn patties and broil 6 to 8 minutes longer. Serve in toasted hamburger buns. Top burgers with additional hot sauerkraut, if desired. Makes 6 sandwiches.

Lamb and Bacon Whirls

Preheat broiler. Combine ½ cup crushed cornflakes; 2 tablespoons water; 1 teaspoon Worcestershire sauce; ½ teaspoon salt; ¼ teaspoon dried marjoram, crushed; and dash pepper. Mix in 1½ pounds ground lamb. Form into 6 patties, 1½ inches thick. Wrap edge of *each* in one slice of bacon; fasten with wooden pick. Broil 3 to 4 inches from heat for 7 to 8 minutes on *each* side, turning once. Serves 6.

Broiled Deviled Burgers

Preheat broiler. Combine ¼ cup catsup, 2 teaspoons prepared horseradish, 2 teaspoons finely chopped onion, 1½ teaspoons prepared mustard, 1½ teaspoons Worcestershire sauce, ¾ teaspoon salt, and dash pepper. Add 1 pound ground beef; mix well. Split 6 hamburger buns and toast *uncut* surfaces under broiler. Spread cut sides with beef mixture. Broil 3 inches from heat for 6 minutes. Makes 6 servings.

For a quick lunch or supper, serve *Tangy Kraut Burgers,* juicy patties of ground beef flavored with sauerkraut. Garnish with cherry tomatoes.

Out of the Salad Bowl

Tomato-Tuna Cups

    1 6½- or 7-ounce can tuna, chilled,
       drained, and flaked
    ½ cup chopped celery
    ⅓ cup fresh or frozen chopped
       green pepper
    2 tablespoons fresh or frozen
       chopped onion
    ½ to 1 teaspoon curry powder
    ¼ teaspoon salt
      Dash pepper
    ½ cup mayonnaise
    6 tomatoes
      Lettuce cups

Combine flaked tuna, chopped celery, chopped green pepper, chopped onion, curry powder, salt, and pepper. Add mayonnaise; toss lightly. With stem end down, cut each tomato into 6 wedges, *cutting to but not through base* of tomato. Spread wedges apart slightly. Sprinkle tomatoes lightly with salt. Fill with tuna mixture. Serve in lettuce cups. Makes 6 servings.

Salami-Cheese Toss

    6 cups torn lettuce
    1 cup thinly sliced small salami
       (6 ounces)
    ½ cup shredded natural Cheddar
       cheese (2 ounces)
    ¼ cup sliced pimiento-stuffed
       green olives
         • • •
    ½ cup Italian salad dressing
    1 teaspoon prepared horseradish
      Dash Worcestershire sauce

In bowl combine lettuce, salami, shredded cheese, and sliced olives. For dressing, stir together Italian salad dressing, prepared horseradish, and Worcestershire sauce; pour dressing over lettuce mixture and toss lightly. Makes 6 to 8 servings.

Chili Con Carne Salad

    1 medium head lettuce
    3 cups corn chips
    4 ounces pepperoni, thinly sliced
    1 large tomato, chopped
    ½ cup shredded natural Cheddar
       cheese (2 ounces)
    ¼ cup sliced ripe olives
    1 15-ounce can chili con carne
       with beans

Line salad bowl with outer lettuce leaves; cut remaining lettuce into chunks. Place lettuce chunks, chips, pepperoni, tomato, cheese, and olives in bowl. Heat chili. Pour atop salad; toss lightly. Serves 6.

Corned Beef-Potato Salad

    2 16-ounce cans sliced potatoes,
       chilled and drained
    1 12-ounce can corned beef, chilled
       and diced
    2 tablespoons chopped green onion
       with tops
    2 hard-cooked eggs, chopped
    ½ cup mayonnaise or salad dressing
    2 tablespoons French salad dressing
    ½ teaspoon celery seed
    ¼ teaspoon salt

In bowl combine potatoes, corned beef, green onion, and hard-cooked eggs. Combine mayonnaise, French dressing, celery seed, and salt; toss with potato-corned beef mixture. Makes 6 servings.

Hearty main dish salad

Toss lettuce, corn chips, tomato, pepperoni, cheese, and olives with hot chili for *Chili Con Carne Salad*. All that's needed to complete the meal is a bread, dessert, and beverage. →

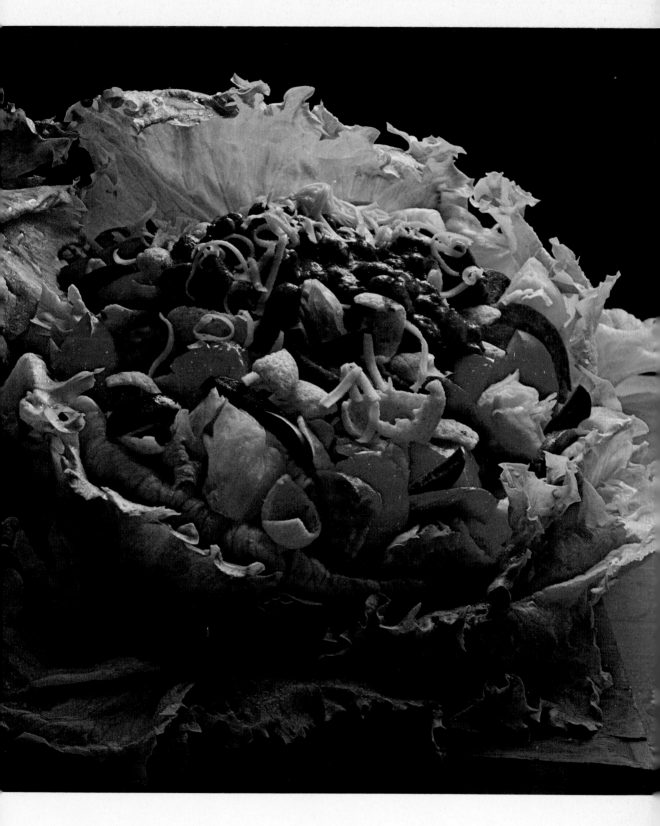

Delight luncheon guests with *Expert Chef's Salad Bowl*. This attractive salad features ham, cheese, avocado, lettuce, and a tangy dressing.

Expert Chef's Salad Bowl

Filling enough to be a meal by itself—

4 cups torn lettuce
2 cups fully cooked ham cut in
    thin strips
2 ounces smoked Cheddar cheese,
    cut into thin strips
1 avocado, peeled and sliced
    into rings
• • •
1 cup salad oil
⅓ cup vinegar
2 tablespoons catsup
1 tablespoon lemon juice
1 teaspoon salt
½ teaspoon paprika
¼ teaspoon sugar
¼ teaspoon pepper

Place lettuce in salad bowl. Arrange ham and cheese spoke-fashion atop lettuce. Arrange avocado rings down center (halve avocado rings, if desired). In screw-top jar combine oil, vinegar, catsup, lemon juice, salt, paprika, sugar, and pepper. Cover and shake vigorously to blend. Serve with salad. Makes 6 servings.

Tuna-Fruit Salad

1 16-ounce can grapefruit and orange
    sections, chilled and drained
1 13½-ounce can pineapple tidbits,
    chilled and drained
1 6½- or 7-ounce can tuna, chilled,
    drained, and flaked
⅓ cup coarsely chopped walnuts
⅓ cup mayonnaise or salad dressing

Combine grapefruit and orange sections, pineapple tidbits, tuna, and walnuts. Add mayonnaise or salad dressing to fruit-tuna mixture and toss lightly. Serves 4.

Ham and Orange Salad

2 cups cubed fully cooked ham
1 cup sliced celery
1 11-ounce can mandarin orange
    sections, chilled and drained
½ cup mayonnaise or salad dressing
2 teaspoons prepared mustard
    Dash *each* salt and pepper
    Lettuce cups

Combine ham, celery, and mandarin oranges. Blend mayonnaise, mustard, salt, and pepper; stir lightly into ham mixture. Serve in lettuce cups. Makes 4 servings.

Chicken Toss

Pea pods add crunch to this tasty salad—

1 6-ounce package frozen pea pods
2 5-ounce cans boned chicken,
    chilled
1 16-ounce can chop suey vegetables,
    chilled, drained, and rinsed
⅓ cup mayonnaise or salad dressing
2 tablespoons soy sauce
    Dash pepper

Pour boiling water over frozen pea pods; let stand 2 minutes, then drain. Meanwhile, cut up chicken. Combine the pea pods, chicken, and chop suey vegetables. Blend the mayonnaise, soy sauce, and pepper; toss with chicken mixture. Serves 4.

Ham-Pineapple Salad

6 cups torn lettuce
2 medium tomatoes, cut in wedges
• • •
2 tablespoons finely chopped onion
1 tablespoon cooking oil
1 tablespoon cornstarch
½ teaspoon salt
Dash pepper
1 13½-ounce can pineapple tidbits
¼ cup packed brown sugar
2 tablespoons vinegar
8 ounces fully cooked ham, cut in
julienne strips (2 cups)

Divide torn lettuce and tomato wedges among six individual salad bowls. In medium saucepan cook finely chopped onion in cooking oil till tender but not brown. Blend in cornstarch, salt, and pepper. Drain pineapple tidbits, reserving syrup. Add syrup to saucepan all at once. Cook, stirring constantly, till mixture is thickened and bubbly. Stir in brown sugar and vinegar; add pineapple tidbits and ham strips. Heat through. Pour hot ham mixture over lettuce mixture. Toss gently till lettuce is coated. Serve immediately. Makes 6 servings.

Western Salad Bowl

2 cups torn lettuce
2 cups torn romaine, chicory, *or*
endive
1½ cups cubed cooked chicken
1 medium tomato, chopped
1 medium avocado, sliced
2 hard-cooked eggs, diced
¼ cup crumbled blue cheese (1 ounce)
Salt
Freshly ground pepper
½ cup garlic salad dressing

In medium salad bowl combine lettuce and romaine, chicory, *or* endive. Arrange cubed chicken, chopped tomato, sliced avocado, diced hard-cooked eggs, and crumbled blue cheese over greens. Season with salt and freshly ground pepper. Toss lightly with garlic salad dressing. Serves 4 or 5.

Shrimp-Macaroni Salad

Keep all the ingredients needed for this delicious salad on hand so you can use it as a last-minute main dish—

1 16-ounce can macaroni and cheese,
chilled
2 4½-ounce cans shrimp, chilled
and drained
1 8-ounce can peas, chilled
and drained
¼ cup mayonnaise or salad dressing
1 tablespoon chopped canned
pimiento
1 teaspoon instant minced onion
Dash bottled hot pepper sauce
Lettuce cups

Using a long-bladed knife, cut macaroni into shorter pieces while in the can. Combine macaroni and cheese, shrimp, peas, mayonnaise or salad dressing, chopped pimiento, instant minced onion, and bottled hot pepper sauce; mix thoroughly. Serve salad in lettuce cups. Makes 4 servings.

Main Dish Salad Bowl

½ cup salad oil
⅓ cup wine vinegar
1 teaspoon instant minced onion
½ teaspoon sugar
½ teaspoon Worcestershire sauce
¼ teaspoon salt
Dash pepper
4 cups torn lettuce
2 cups torn curly endive
1 12-ounce can chopped ham, cut
in strips
¼ cup crumbled blue cheese (1 ounce)
1 medium tomato, cut in wedges

In screw-top jar combine salad oil, wine vinegar, instant minced onion, sugar, Worcestershire sauce, salt, and pepper; cover and shake vigorously till blended. In salad bowl combine torn lettuce, torn curly endive, strips of chopped ham, blue cheese, and tomato wedges. Shake dressing again to blend; pour over salad, tossing to coat all ingredients. Makes 6 servings.

Off the Breadboard

Ham Sandwich Deluxe

This fancy sandwich is pictured on page 46—

> 1 oblong loaf rye bread, about 12
>   inches long
> 2 tablespoons butter or margarine
> 1 4-ounce container whipped
>   cream cheese
> 1 6-ounce package ham salad
> ¼ cup chopped ripe olives
> ¼ cup sliced radishes
> 3 hard-cooked eggs, sliced

Cut two ¾-inch-thick slices from center of rye loaf. (Use remaining bread elsewhere.) Spread *each* slice bread with *half* the butter or margarine and *half* the cream cheese. Place *half* the ham salad in center of *each* slice; surround with a ring of olives and a ring of radishes. Arrange row of egg slices down center of *each*. Garnish with parsley, if desired. Cut each sandwich in half to serve. Makes 4 servings.

Braunschweiger Special

> 1 4-ounce container whipped
>   cream cheese
> 2 tablespoons mayonnaise or
>   salad dressing
>   Several drops bottled hot pepper
>   sauce
> 12 slices whole wheat bread
> 12 slices braunschweiger, thinly
>   sliced (12 ounces)
> ½ of a 3½-ounce can French-fried
>   onions, crumbled
>   Lettuce

Combine whipped cream cheese, mayonnaise, and hot pepper sauce; spread on *one side of each* slice of bread. Top *each of 6* bread slices with 2 braunschweiger slices; sprinkle with crumbled onions. Top with lettuce. Cover with remaining bread, cream cheese side in. Makes 6 servings.

Surf Boards

Filled with a seafood mixture—

> 6 individual French rolls
> 2 tablespoons butter, softened
> 1 7½-ounce can crab meat, drained,
>   flaked, and cartilage removed
> 1 4½-ounce can shrimp, drained
> 1 cup diced celery
> ¾ cup mayonnaise or salad dressing
> ¼ cup sweet pickle relish
> 2 tablespoons finely chopped onion
> 1 tablespoon lemon juice
> ½ teaspoon salt
> ½ teaspoon Worcestershire
>   sauce
>   Dash pepper

Split rolls lengthwise; spread with butter. Combine remaining ingredients. Spread mixture on bottom halves of rolls; cover with roll tops. Makes 6 servings.

Salmon Club Sandwiches

> ½ cup mayonnaise or salad dressing
> ½ cup finely chopped celery
> 1 teaspoon instant minced onion
> ¼ teaspoon prepared mustard
> 1 7¾-ounce can salmon, drained and
>   flaked
> ½ cup cream-style cottage cheese
> 2 tablespoons sweet pickle relish
> ¼ teaspoon dried dillweed, crushed
> 12 slices bread, toasted and buttered
> 4 lettuce leaves

Combine mayonnaise or salad dressing, celery, onion, and mustard; stir in salmon. Combine cottage cheese, pickle relish, and dillweed. Spread 4 slices of toast with salmon mixture; top *each* with second slice of toast, lettuce leaf, *one-fourth* of cottage cheese mixture, and another slice of toast. Cut each sandwich in quarters; secure with wooden picks. Makes 4 servings.

Ham and Egg Salad Sandwiches

1 cup diced fully cooked ham
2 hard-cooked eggs, chopped
1 tablespoon finely chopped
    green onion
⅓ cup mayonnaise or salad dressing
2 teaspoons prepared mustard
    • • •
4 to 6 individual French rolls, split
Lettuce

In bowl combine ham, chopped egg, and onion. Stir in mayonnaise and mustard. Spoon into French rolls lined with lettuce. Makes 4 to 6 servings.

Ham-Slaw Sandwiches

2 cups finely shredded cabbage
¼ teaspoon celery seed
½ cup blue cheese salad dressing
4 or 8 slices dark rye bread,
    buttered
8 slices boiled ham
1 medium avocado, seeded, peeled,
    and sliced

Combine cabbage and celery seed; toss with enough dressing to moisten. On *each of 4 slices* bread arrange some cabbage mixture, 2 slices ham, and avocado. Serve open face *or* top with remaining bread. Serves 4.

Double decker *Salmon Club Sandwiches* offer two unique fillings. The cottage cheese layer is seasoned with pickle relish and dillweed. Celery and a hint of mustard enhance the zesty salmon layer.

From Planned Overs

Ham and Cheese Scramble

1 cup cubed fully cooked ham
1 tablespoon chopped green onion
3 tablespoons butter or margarine
1 cup cream-style cottage cheese
6 eggs
1 cup canned shoestring potatoes

In skillet cook ham and green onion in butter till lightly browned. Drain cottage cheese, reserving liquid. Add reserved liquid and dash pepper to eggs; beat. Pour egg mixture into skillet with ham and onion. Cook over low heat. When mixture begins to set at bottom and sides, lift cooked portion with wide spatula so uncooked mixture goes to bottom of skillet. Continue cooking till eggs are cooked through but still moist and glossy, 5 to 8 minutes. Fold in cottage cheese; remove from skillet immediately. Spoon onto shoestring potatoes. Makes 4 servings.

Easy Beef Stew

2 tablespoons butter or margarine
2 tablespoons all-purpose flour
1 8-ounce can tomato sauce
½ cup dry red wine
2 cups cubed cooked beef
1 11½-ounce can sliced carrots
1 tablespoon instant minced onion
½ teaspoon dried thyme, crushed
¼ teaspoon garlic salt
¼ teaspoon salt
⅛ teaspoon ground cinnamon
1 2-inch strip orange peel
Hot cooked noodles

In large saucepan melt butter; stir in flour. Add tomato sauce, wine, and ¾ cup water. Cook and stir till thickened. Add beef, undrained carrots, onion, thyme, garlic salt, salt, cinnamon, and orange peel. Cover; simmer about 15 minutes. Serve over hot cooked noodles. Serves 4 to 6.

Meat Loaf-Stuffed Tomatoes

This attractive dish is shown on page 4 —

4 large tomatoes
4 slices sharp process American cheese
1½ cups crumbled cooked meat loaf or meatballs
1 8-ounce can kidney beans, drained
2 tablespoons chili sauce
1½ teaspoons chili powder

Preheat broiler. Cut off tops of tomatoes; scoop out pulp and invert shells to drain. Chop 1 cup pulp; drain well. Cut cheese slices in quarters diagonally. In saucepan combine *half* the cheese, chopped tomato pulp, crumbled meat loaf, kidney beans, chili sauce, and chili powder. Simmer 10 minutes. Meanwhile, generously salt inside of tomato shells. Broil 4 inches from heat till hot, about 3 minutes. Stuff tomatoes with meat mixture. Top *each* with 2 of the remaining cheese quarters. Broil till cheese melts. Makes 4 servings.

Peach and Chicken Cups

½ cup dairy sour cream
¼ cup mayonnaise or salad dressing
½ teaspoon dried thyme, crushed
¼ teaspoon dried basil, crushed
Dash sugar
Dash *each* salt and pepper
2 cups cubed cooked chicken
1 8¾-ounce can peach slices, chilled, drained, and diced
½ cup garlic-flavored croutons
4 thick rings green pepper

Combine sour cream, mayonnaise, thyme, basil, sugar, salt, and pepper. Add chicken and peaches, tossing to coat. Fold in croutons. Spoon chicken mixture into green pepper rings; garnish with additional peach slices, if desired. Serves 4.

Oyster-Rice Casserole

2 cups cooked rice
1 6-ounce can evaporated milk
  (⅔ cup)
½ cup finely chopped celery
¼ cup finely chopped onion
1 5-ounce can oysters, drained
1 2-ounce package seasoned coating
  mix for fish
2 tablespoons butter or margarine

Preheat oven to 400°. Combine first 4 ingredients and ½ teaspoon salt; turn into 1-quart casserole. Make well in center of mixture. Place oysters and coating mix in plastic bag; shake to coat oysters. Place oysters and remaining coating mix atop rice; dot with butter. Bake at 400° till oysters are golden and mixture is heated through, 20 to 25 minutes. Makes 4 servings.

Sweet-Sour Pork

2 cups cubed cooked pork
½ cup fresh or frozen chopped onion
1 clove garlic, minced
2 tablespoons cooking oil
1 13¼-ounce can pineapple chunks
2 tablespoons red wine vinegar
2 tablespoons soy sauce
1 tablespoon packed brown sugar
1 chicken bouillon cube
3 tablespoons cold water
2 tablespoons cornstarch
1 small green pepper, cut in strips
1 tomato, cut in wedges
  Hot cooked rice

Cook pork, onion, and garlic in hot oil till onion is tender. Drain pineapple, reserving syrup. Add reserved syrup, vinegar, soy sauce, brown sugar, bouillon cube, and 1 cup water to skillet. Simmer, covered, 15 minutes. Blend 3 tablespoons cold water and cornstarch; stir into pork mixture. Cook and stir till thick and bubbly. Add pineapple and green pepper; cook over low heat just till green pepper is crisp-tender, 2 to 3 minutes. Add tomato; heat through. Serve over rice. Makes 4 servings.

Fruited Turkey Sandwiches

A delicious and pretty open-faced sandwich—

4 slices raisin bread, toasted
  Butter or margarine
½ cup whole cranberry sauce
4 slices cooked turkey
4 slices process Swiss cheese
1 8¼-ounce can pineapple slices,
  well drained (4 slices)

Preheat broiler. Spread one side of each slice toast with butter. Then, spread with cranberry sauce. Top *each* with a turkey slice, cheese slice, and pineapple slice. Broil 3 inches from heat till cheese is melted, 3 to 4 minutes. Makes 4.

Broiled Pork Sandwiches

2 English muffins, split and toasted
8 very thin slices cooked pork
4 slices sharp process American
  cheese, cut in half
½ cup applesauce
  Ground cinnamon (optional)

Preheat broiler. On *each* muffin half, place 2 slices pork and half slice cheese. Spoon 2 tablespoons applesauce atop *each;* sprinkle lightly with cinnamon, if desired. Broil 3 to 4 inches from heat for 1½ to 2 minutes. Top *each* with one of the remaining half slices cheese. Broil till lightly browned, about 1½ minutes. Makes 4 sandwiches.

Hot Roast Beef Sandwiches

1 cup catsup
2 tablespoons packed brown sugar
2 tablespoons steak sauce
½ teaspoon dry mustard
16 ounces very thinly sliced cooked
  roast beef
4 hamburger buns, split and toasted

In saucepan combine catsup, brown sugar, steak sauce, dry mustard, and ½ teaspoon salt; add beef. Cover; simmer 10 to 15 minutes. Spoon onto buns. Serves 4.

Often, in the rush of preparing a meal, the main dish accompaniments are forgotten and soon you're in a rut of serving lettuce wedges, buttered vegetables, purchased bread, and ice cream. It's time to put new life into your meals.

The speedy *salad, vegetable, bread,* and *dessert* recipes in this section will help you do just that. Select from the many fruit and vegetable salads, vegetable dress-ups including potato dishes, tasty breads, coffee cakes, cupcakes, compotes, and other desserts. You'll find an accompaniment for any main dish.

And, to make sure that the whole meal will be quick to prepare, refer to the Main Dish Preparation Times on page 92.

Rounding Out The Meal

From left: *Apricot Mousse, Orange-Ginger Sauce* over vanilla ice cream, *Pink Parfaits, Marshmallow Sauce* over lime sherbet. *Zabaglione,* and *Ruby Fruit Compote.* (See page 91 for all recipes.)

Salads

Avocado-Orange Platter

2 medium avocados, peeled and sliced
lengthwise
2 medium oranges, peeled and
sliced
Lettuce leaves
½ cup Italian salad dressing
2 tablespoons sweet pickle relish
1 teaspoon instant minced onion

Just before serving, arrange avocados and oranges on lettuce-lined plate. In screw-top jar combine dressing, relish, and onion; shake. Serve over salad. Serves 4 to 6.

Blender Coleslaw

Sliced cabbage
¼ green pepper, seeded
½ carrot, peeled
1 slice onion
Bottled coleslaw salad dressing

Fill blender container to 3-cup measure with sliced cabbage. Cut vegetables in pieces and add to container; cover with water. Blend on high speed just till vegetables are chopped, about 3 seconds. *Do not overblend.* Drain thoroughly in sieve. Toss with coleslaw dressing. Serves 2.

Tangy Lime Dressing

⅓ cup honey
⅓ cup salad oil
¼ cup frozen limeade concentrate,
thawed
1 teaspoon celery seed
1 drop green food coloring

Combine honey, salad oil, concentrate, celery seed, and green food coloring. Beat with rotary beater till smooth and thickened. Makes about ¾ cup dressing.

Cran-Mandarin Toss

1 envelope creamy French salad
dressing mix
½ teaspoon grated orange peel
8 cups torn mixed salad greens
1 11-ounce can mandarin orange
sections, drained
1 8-ounce can jellied cranberry
sauce, chilled

Prepare salad dressing mix according to package directions, adding grated orange peel; chill. In large salad bowl toss together salad greens and mandarin orange sections. Cut chilled jellied cranberry sauce into cubes; add to salad and mix gently. Pass dressing. Makes 8 servings.

Beet-Egg Salad

1 16-ounce can sliced beets, chilled
and drained
3 hard-cooked eggs, quartered
Lettuce leaves
½ cup mayonnaise or salad dressing
¼ cup chili sauce
1 teaspoon prepared horseradish
¼ teaspoon Worcestershire sauce
⅛ teaspoon garlic salt
Dash pepper

Arrange beets and hard-cooked eggs on lettuce-lined plates. Combine mayonnaise, chili sauce, horseradish, Worcestershire, garlic salt, and pepper. Mix well and serve over salad. Makes 4 servings.

Unusual tossed salad

Mix tangy cubes of jellied cranberry sauce with →
mandarin oranges and salad greens to make colorful *Cran-Mandarin Toss.* To serve, pass the creamy dressing with this unique salad.

Egg and Bean Salad

6 hard-cooked eggs, coarsely chopped
1 14-ounce jar baked beans in
   molasses sauce (1¾ cups)
½ cup sliced celery
2 tablespoons fresh or frozen
   chopped green pepper
1 tablespoon minced onion
1 tablespoon mayonnaise or salad
   dressing
1 tablespoon chili sauce
1 teaspoon vinegar
¾ teaspoon salt
   Dash pepper
   Dash Worcestershire sauce
   Lettuce cups

In bowl combine all ingredients *except* lettuce cups. Mix together lightly and chill till ready to serve. Serve salad in lettuce cups. Garnish with bacon curls, if desired. Makes 6 to 8 servings.

Serve nutritious *Egg and Bean Salad* in crisp lettuce cups. This tasty salad starts with hard-cooked eggs and a jar of baked beans.

Pimiento Salad Bowl

Blue cheese is an unexpected surprise—

1 4-ounce jar pimientos
1 small onion, quartered
⅓ cup salad oil
¼ cup vinegar
2 tablespoons crumbled blue cheese
1½ teaspoons sugar
½ teaspoon salt
4 whole black peppercorns
   • • •
1 small head lettuce, cut in chunks
   (6 cups)
1 medium cucumber, sliced (2 cups)
1 16-ounce can grapefruit sections,
   chilled and drained

In blender container combine undrained pimientos, onion, salad oil, vinegar, crumbled blue cheese, sugar, salt, and whole black peppercorns. Blend at high speed till smooth, about 10 seconds. Place dressing in freezer to chill. Meanwhile, in salad bowl combine lettuce, cucumber slices, and grapefruit sections. Toss lightly with dressing. Makes 6 servings.

Blue-Dressed Tossed Salad

1 cup cream-style cottage cheese
½ cup water
¼ cup crumbled blue cheese (1 ounce)
¼ cup instant nonfat dry milk powder
1 tablespoon lemon juice
¼ teaspoon onion salt
2 tablespoons crumbled blue cheese
8 cups torn fresh spinach
½ medium red onion, thinly sliced
5 slices bacon, crisp-cooked,
   drained, and crumbled

In blender container combine cream-style cottage cheese, water, ¼ cup crumbled blue cheese, instant nonfat dry milk powder, lemon juice, and onion salt. Cover and blend till smooth. Stir in the 2 tablespoons crumbled blue cheese; chill till served. Meanwhile, toss together spinach, red onion, and crumbled bacon; serve with the chilled dressing. Makes 6 servings.

Dutch Boy Lettuce

A wilted spinach-lettuce salad—

    4 slices bacon
    1 slightly beaten egg
    ⅓ cup dairy sour cream
    ¼ cup vinegar
    2 tablespoons sugar
      Dash salt
          • • •
    6 cups torn spinach (½ pound)
    3 cups torn lettuce
    3 to 4 green onions, sliced

In large skillet cook bacon till crisp. Drain bacon, reserving 1 tablespoon drippings in skillet; crumble bacon and set aside. Combine egg, dairy sour cream, vinegar, sugar, and salt; stir into reserved drippings. Cook and stir till thickened. Add spinach, lettuce, and sliced green onions, tossing till coated. Serve immediately. Makes 8 to 10 servings.

Italian-Parmesan Mayonnaise

An easy-to-make tangy salad dressing—

    ½ cup Italian salad dressing
    1 cup mayonnaise or salad dressing
    ¼ cup grated Parmesan cheese

Gradually stir Italian salad dressing into mayonnaise. Add grated Parmesan cheese and mix till well blended. Chill dressing till served. Makes 1½ cups dressing.

French Fruit Dressing

Serve with a fruit salad plate—

    ½ cup sweet French salad dressing
    ½ cup mayonnaise or salad dressing
    ¼ cup pineapple juice
    1 tablespoon blue cheese salad
        dressing mix

In small mixing bowl combine sweet French salad dressing, mayonnaise or salad dressing, pineapple juice, and dry blue cheese salad dressing mix. Beat with rotary beater till smooth; chill dressing till served. Makes about 1¼ cups dressing.

Calypso Dressing

Good served over fresh or canned fruits—

    1 large banana, sliced
    1 cup fresh or frozen cranberries
    1 cup pineapple yogurt
    ½ cup mayonnaise or salad dressing
    ¼ cup sugar
    ¼ teaspoon ground ginger

In blender container combine sliced banana and cranberries. Cover and blend till finely chopped, stopping to scrape mixture down sides of container when necessary. Turn into bowl and stir in pineapple yogurt, mayonnaise or salad dressing, sugar, and ground ginger. Chill till served. Makes about 2½ cups salad dressing.

Tomato Pinwheel

For each serving, cut a ½-inch-thick slice from a head of lettuce. Place on salad plate and top with a creamy-type salad dressing, such as thousand island or green goddess salad dressing. Cut one tomato half into 4 or 5 wedges; arrange in a pinwheel design over dressing. Garnish salad with parsley or watercress.

Jiffy Peach Salad

    1 5-ounce jar Neufchâtel cheese
        spread with pimiento
    1 3-ounce package cream cheese,
        softened
    ½ cup mayonnaise or salad dressing
    1 22-ounce can peach pie filling
    1 11-ounce can mandarin orange
        sections, drained
    1 8½-ounce can pineapple
        tidbits, drained
    1 cup miniature marshmallows
      Lettuce

Beat together cheese spread, cream cheese, and mayonnaise; fold in peach pie filling, fruits, and marshmallows. Chill till served. Serve in lettuce-lined bowl or lettuce cups. Makes 10 servings.

Vegetables

Cheesy Potatoes

⅓ cup milk
1 10½-ounce can condensed cream of
  celery soup
2 16-ounce cans whole new potatoes,
  drained
1 3-ounce can sliced mushrooms,
  drained
1 cup shredded natural Cheddar
  cheese (4 ounces)

In saucepan stir milk into soup. Add potatoes and mushrooms; heat. Stir in cheese; heat and stir till melted. Serves 6.

Honey-Ginger Carrots

2 tablespoons butter or margarine
3 tablespoons honey
2 tablespoons packed brown sugar
⅛ teaspoon ground ginger
2 16-ounce cans sliced carrots,
  drained

In skillet melt butter. Add honey, brown sugar, and ginger; heat and stir till bubbly. Add carrots; cook, turning frequently, till heated through and glazed. Serve in sauce dishes. Makes 8 servings.

Wine-Sauced Potatoes

½ of a 24-ounce package frozen
  hashed brown potatoes with
  onion and peppers (3 cups)
2 tablespoons butter or margarine
2 tablespoons all-purpose flour
1 cup milk
2 tablespoons dry white wine

Cook potatoes in butter till soft. Stir in flour and ½ teaspoon salt; add milk all at once. Cook and stir till thickened and bubbly. Stir in wine. Serves 4.

Asparagus with Two-Cheese Sauce

Fresh asparagus
1 3-ounce package cream
  cheese, softened
½ cup evaporated milk
2 tablespoons grated Parmesan cheese

Cook asparagus, covered, in small amount of boiling salted water for 10 to 15 minutes; drain. Meanwhile, in small saucepan beat cream cheese till smooth; gradually beat in evaporated milk. Cook and stir till hot, 3 to 5 minutes. Stir in *1 tablespoon* of the Parmesan and dash salt. Pour over hot asparagus; sprinkle with remaining Parmesan. Makes ¾ cup sauce.

Brown Rice

In 4-quart pressure cooker combine 2 cups water, 1 cup brown rice, and ½ teaspoon salt; cover tightly. Put pressure regulator in place. Cook 15 minutes with pressure regulator rocking gently (15 pounds pressure). Cool quickly under cold running water. Makes 3 cups rice.

Quick Baked Potatoes

4 *small* baking potatoes
¼ cup butter or margarine, melted
Salt
Onion powder
Garlic powder
Paprika

Preheat oven to 425°. Halve potatoes lengthwise. Using sharp knife, score cut surfaces in crisscross pattern, but do not cut skins. Place on 15½x10½x1-inch baking pan; drizzle with butter and sprinkle with salt, onion powder, and garlic powder. Bake at 425° for 30 to 35 minutes. Sprinkle with paprika. Serves 4.

Speedy Creamed Potatoes

4 cups cubed raw potatoes
⅓ cup fresh or frozen chopped onion
½ cup light cream
2 tablespoons snipped parsley

In 4-quart pressure cooker combine potatoes, onion, ⅓ cup water, and 1½ teaspoons salt. Close cover securely; cook 2 minutes with pressure regulator rocking gently (15 pounds pressure). Immediately remove from heat; reduce pressure quickly by placing under cold running water. Add cream and parsley. Heat through, uncovered, stirring gently. Makes 6 servings.

Gourmet Onions

Cook 6 medium onions, sliced (3 cups), in 3 tablespoons butter till barely tender but not brown. Stir to separate rings. Add ¼ cup dry sherry, ½ teaspoon *each* sugar and salt, and ⅛ teaspoon pepper. Cook quickly for 2 to 3 minutes. Sprinkle with 2 tablespoons grated Parmesan cheese; serve in sauce dishes. Makes 6 servings.

Cabbage-Carrot Combo

4 cups coarsely shredded cabbage
2 medium carrots, finely shredded
⅓ cup sugar
1 tablespoon all-purpose flour
¾ teaspoon dry mustard
2 beaten eggs
⅓ cup vinegar
¼ cup milk

Combine cabbage and carrots; cook, covered, in boiling salted water for 7 minutes. Drain well. Meanwhile, combine sugar, flour, dry mustard, and ¼ teaspoon salt; add eggs and beat till blended. In small saucepan heat vinegar to boiling. Gradually stir hot vinegar into egg mixture; return to saucepan. Cook, stirring constantly, till thickened and bubbly. Stir in milk; heat through. Pour over vegetables; toss lightly to blend well. Makes 6 servings.

Orangy Beans

1 31-ounce can pork and beans
   in tomato sauce
½ cup packed brown sugar
¼ cup catsup
3 tablespoons frozen orange juice
   concentrate, thawed
1 tablespoon instant minced onion
½ teaspoon Worcestershire sauce

Combine all ingredients; bring to boiling. Simmer, uncovered, for 10 minutes, stirring occasionally. Makes 6 to 8 servings.

Broccoli Especial

Cook one 10-ounce package frozen broccoli spears according to package directions. In small saucepan combine 2 tablespoons chopped canned pimiento; 2 tablespoons capers, drained; and 2 tablespoons Italian salad dressing; heat through. Pour dressing mixture over hot broccoli. Serves 4.

Flavorful *Orangy Beans* are a saucepan version of baked beans. They are easy to make using canned beans and frozen juice concentrate.

Breads

Bran Muffins

Use a blender to mix these in a jiffy—

1⅓ cups all-purpose flour
1 cup bran flakes
¼ cup packed brown sugar
1 teaspoon baking soda
½ teaspoon salt

• • •

1 cup dairy sour cream
1 egg
¼ cup molasses
¼ cup cooking oil
½ teaspoon vanilla

Preheat oven to 400°. In mixing bowl thoroughly stir together flour, bran flakes, brown sugar, soda, and salt. In blender container combine sour cream, egg, molasses, oil, and vanilla; blend to combine. Pour sour cream mixture over dry ingredients; stir just till combined. Fill greased muffin pans ⅔ full. Bake at 400° for 15 to 18 minutes. Makes 12 muffins.

Orange Coffee Cake

3 tablespoons sugar
2 tablespoons all-purpose flour
½ teaspoon ground cinnamon
2 tablespoons butter or margarine, softened
2 tablespoons chopped nuts

• • •

1 14-ounce package orange muffin mix
2 tablespoons apricot preserves

Preheat oven to 400°. Stir together sugar, flour, and cinnamon. Cut in butter till mixture is in fine crumbs; stir in nuts. Prepare muffin mix according to package directions. Spread batter into greased 9x1½-inch round baking pan. Sprinkle nut mixture over; dot with apricot preserves. Bake at 400° till golden brown, 20 to 25 minutes. Makes 1 coffee cake.

Onion-Cheese Supper Bread

Snipped parsley adds a pretty touch—

½ cup fresh or frozen chopped onion
1 tablespoon butter or margarine
1 beaten egg
½ cup milk
1½ cups packaged biscuit mix

• • •

1 cup shredded sharp process American cheese (4 ounces)
2 tablespoons snipped parsley

Preheat oven to 400°. In skillet cook onion in butter till tender but not brown. Combine beaten egg and milk; add to packaged biscuit mix. Stir only till biscuit mix is moistened. Add cooked onion, *half* of the process American cheese, and snipped parsley. Spread dough in greased 8x1½-inch round baking pan. Sprinkle dough with the remaining American cheese. Bake at 400° till wooden pick comes out clean, 20 to 25 minutes. Makes 6 to 8 servings.

Barbecue Biscuits

Chili sauce, Worcestershire, and onion combine to make these biscuits spicy hot—

¼ cup chili sauce
¼ cup milk
1 teaspoon snipped parsley
1 teaspoon Worcestershire sauce
½ teaspoon instant minced onion
2 cups packaged biscuit mix

Preheat oven to 450°. In mixing bowl combine chili sauce, milk, snipped parsley, Worcestershire sauce, and instant minced onion; let mixture stand 5 minutes. Stir in packaged biscuit mix to make a soft dough. Form dough into a ball on floured surface; knead 5 times. Roll to ½-inch thickness; cut into 2-inch rounds. Bake on ungreased baking sheet at 450° for 8 to 10 minutes. Makes 10 to 12 biscuits.

Garlic Breadsticks

Easy to make using frankfurter buns—

½ cup butter or margarine
½ teaspoon garlic powder
4 frankfurter buns, split
2 tablespoons sesame seed

Preheat oven to 450°. Combine butter and garlic powder in 13x9x2-inch baking pan. Heat in oven till butter melts. Meanwhile, split *each bun half* lengthwise, making a total of 16 pieces. Quickly dip each piece in melted butter; set aside till all are coated. Arrange in baking pan so pieces do not touch. Sprinkle with sesame seed. Toast in 450° oven till golden, about 10 minutes. Makes 16 breadsticks.

Parmesan Slices

¼ cup butter or margarine, softened
¼ cup grated Parmesan cheese
6 slices French or Vienna bread, cut 1 inch thick
1 teaspoon poppy seed (optional)

Preheat oven to 425°. Combine butter and Parmesan; spread on both sides of bread. Sprinkle with poppy seed, if desired. Place on baking sheet; toast at 425° for 5 to 6 minutes, turning once. Serves 6.

Zippy French Loaves

1 3-ounce package cream cheese with chives, softened
2 tablespoons butter or margarine, softened
1 teaspoon prepared horseradish
1 10-ounce package brown-and-serve French bread (2 loaves)

Preheat oven to 400°. Combine cream cheese with chives, butter or margarine, and horseradish. Cut each loaf of French bread diagonally into slices, *cutting to but not through* bottom crust. Spread butter mixture between slices. Bake on baking sheet at 400° till browned, 12 to 15 minutes.

To make festive, pecan-topped *Blintz Bubble Ring,* layer balls of refrigerated biscuit dough filled with cream cheese and cinnamon sugar.

Blintz Bubble Ring

2 3-ounce packages cream cheese
2 packages refrigerated biscuits (20 biscuits)
½ cup sugar
1 teaspoon ground cinnamon
3 tablespoons butter or margarine, melted
⅓ cup chopped pecans

Preheat oven to 375°. Cut cream cheese into 20 pieces; shape each into a ball. Roll each refrigerated biscuit to about 3 inches in diameter. Combine sugar and cinnamon. Place one cheese ball and 1 teaspoon cinnamon mixture on each biscuit; bring up edges of dough and pinch to seal. Pour melted butter into bottom of 5-cup ring mold. Sprinkle *half* the pecans and *half* the remaining cinnamon mixture into mold. Place *half* the filled biscuits atop mixture, seam side up; repeat layers. Bake at 375° till browned, about 20 minutes. Cool 5 minutes in pan; invert onto serving plate. Makes 1 coffee cake.

Desserts

Speedy Chocolate Bavarian

1 envelope unflavored gelatin
1 tablespoon sugar
2 teaspoons instant coffee powder
½ cup boiling water
1 6-ounce package semisweet
    chocolate pieces (1 cup)
½ teaspoon vanilla
2 egg yolks
1 cup whipping cream
¾ cup finely crushed ice, *drained*

Put first 3 ingredients, ¼ cup cold water, and dash salt in blender container. Let stand 2 minutes. Add boiling water; cover and blend at high speed till gelatin is dissolved, about 40 seconds. Add chocolate pieces and vanilla. Cover; blend at high speed till smooth, about 10 seconds. Keeping motor running on low speed, remove cover; add yolks, cream, and ice. Blend till mixture begins to thicken, about 20 seconds more. Pour into sherbets; chill at least 10 minutes. Makes 6 servings.

Blueberry-Sauced Waffles

12 frozen waffles
½ cup sugar
4 teaspoons cornstarch
¼ teaspoon ground nutmeg
1½ cups frozen unsweetened
    blueberries
2 tablespoons lemon juice
    Vanilla ice cream

Heat frozen waffles according to package directions for oven method. Meanwhile, in saucepan combine sugar, cornstarch, and nutmeg; stir in ½ cup water. Add frozen blueberries. Cook and stir till thick and bubbly, crushing berries slightly. Remove from heat; stir in lemon juice. Top waffles with scoop of ice cream and drizzle with warm blueberry sauce. Serves 6.

Ginger Waffles

3 cups finely crushed gingersnaps
4 teaspoons baking powder
3 beaten egg yolks
1 cup milk
¼ cup butter, melted
3 egg whites
    Citrus Sauce
    Whipped cream

Preheat waffle baker. In bowl combine crushed gingersnaps, baking powder, and ½ teaspoon salt. Combine yolks, milk, and butter; stir into crumb mixture. Beat egg whites till stiff peaks form; fold into egg yolk mixture just till combined. Bake in waffle baker. Serve warm with Citrus Sauce and whipped cream. Makes 14 waffles.

Citrus Sauce: Combine ½ cup sugar, 2 tablespoons cornstarch, and dash salt. Stir in ¾ cup water; bring to boiling. Cook and stir till bubbly. Stir in ½ teaspoon *each* grated orange and lemon peel, ½ cup orange juice, 1 tablespoon lemon juice, and 1 tablespoon butter; heat through. Serve warm. Makes 1⅓ cups.

Self-Filled Cupcakes

1 8-ounce package cream cheese,
    softened
⅓ cup sugar
1 egg
1 6-ounce package semisweet
    chocolate pieces (1 cup)
1 package chocolate cake mix
    (enough for a 2-layer cake)

Cream the cheese with sugar; beat in egg and dash salt. Stir in chocolate pieces. Set aside. Prepare cake mix according to package directions; fill paper bake cup-lined muffin pans ⅔ full. Drop one rounded teaspoonful cheese mixture into each cupcake. Bake as package directs. Makes 30.

Mix up gingersnap batter and bake elegant *Ginger Waffles* for dessert. Drizzle with tangy lemon-orange sauce. Or, heat frozen waffles for *Blueberry-Sauced Waffles;* top with nutmeg-flavored blueberry sauce.

Fresh Pineapple Dessert

   1 medium fully ripe fresh pineapple
   2 tablespoons sifted powdered sugar
   1 bunch red grapes

With sharp knife, quarter pineapple lengthwise, cutting through crown but leaving it attached. Remove core. Using a sharp knife, loosen fruit from shell but do not remove. Slice through fruit at ½-inch intervals. Sprinkle with powdered sugar. Place on plates; add grapes. Garnish with fresh mint sprigs, if desired. Serves 4.

Chilled Prune Whip

Next time, use another flavor of baby food—

   3 egg whites
   ⅓ cup sugar
   2 4½-ounce jars or cans strained
       prunes (baby food)
   2 tablespoons lemon juice

Beat egg whites till soft peaks form. Gradually add sugar, beating till stiff peaks form. Combine prunes and lemon juice; fold into egg whites. Spoon into 6 sherbets; chill till served. Serves 6.

Strawberry Meringue Puffs

> 2 egg whites
> ½ teaspoon vanilla
> ½ cup sugar
> 4 sponge cake dessert cups
> 1 pint strawberry ice cream
> 1 10-ounce package frozen
>   strawberries, thawed

Preheat oven to 450°. Beat egg whites and vanilla till soft peaks form. Gradually add sugar, beating till stiff peaks form. Spread meringue on tops and sides of dessert cups. Place on baking sheet; bake at 450° about 5 minutes. To serve, top with ice cream; spoon berries over. Serves 4.

Coffee-Cream Topping

Beat 2 cups whipping cream with ½ cup sifted powdered sugar, 2 teaspoons instant coffee powder, and 1 teaspoon vanilla just till mixture holds peaks. Frost top and sides of one 8-inch angel cake or spoon atop cake slices. Serves 10 to 12.

Try delicate *Strawberry Meringue Puffs* for a double strawberry treat. Top dessert cups with strawberry ice cream and plump red berries.

1-2-3 Crème Brûlée

> 1 3⅝- or 3¾-ounce package *instant*
>   vanilla pudding mix
> 1½ cups milk
> ½ cup frozen whipped dessert
>   topping, thawed
> ¼ cup packed brown sugar

Prepare pudding according to package directions, *except* use 1½ cups milk. Fold topping into pudding; spoon into 6 custard cups. Chill at least 10 minutes. Sprinkle *each* with 2 teaspoons brown sugar. Place in shallow pan and surround with ice cubes and a little cold water. Watching closely, broil about 5 inches from heat till bubbly brown crust forms, about 2 minutes. Serve immediately. Makes 6 servings.

Peach Petal Pie

Preheat oven to 350°. Mix one 21-ounce can peach pie filling, 2 tablespoons butter, ⅛ teaspoon ground cinnamon, and a few drops almond extract. Cook and stir till bubbly; pour into 8-inch pie plate. Overlap ten ½-inch-thick slices refrigerated slice-and-bake sugar cookies around edge of pie plate. Mix 1 teaspoon sugar and dash ground cinnamon; sprinkle over cookies. Bake at 350° about 20 minutes. Serve warm with vanilla ice cream. Serves 5 or 6.

Three-Fruit Combo

> 1 13½-ounce can pineapple chunks,
>   chilled
> 1 17-ounce can pitted light sweet
>   cherries, chilled and drained
> 1 11-ounce can mandarin orange
>   sections, chilled and drained
> ½ cup peach preserves
> ¼ teaspoon ground cinnamon

Drain pineapple, reserving 2 tablespoons syrup. Combine pineapple, cherries, and mandarin oranges. Stir together preserves, reserved syrup, and cinnamon; drizzle over fruits. Chill till served. Makes 6 servings.

Pink Parfaits

1 3-ounce package strawberry-
  flavored gelatin
¾ cup boiling water
1 10-ounce package frozen
  sliced strawberries
1 cup strawberry ice cream

In blender container combine gelatin and boiling water. Cover and blend at high speed till gelatin is dissolved, about 20 seconds. Cut package of frozen strawberries in half; allow *half* to thaw for topping. Add remaining strawberries to gelatin; blend till nearly smooth. Add ice cream, a spoonful at a time, blending till smooth after each addition. Pour mixture into 4 parfait glasses; chill in freezer at least 10 minutes. To serve, garnish with thawed strawberries. Makes 4 servings.

Zabaglione

3 egg yolks
¼ cup sugar
¼ cup sweet sherry
2 tablespoons water
  Canned or fresh peach halves

In top of double boiler combine egg yolks, sugar, sherry, and water. Beat till blended. Place over boiling water, but do not touch water. Beat with electric mixer till mixture thickens and mounds like whipped cream, about 5 minutes. Serve immediately over peaches. Makes 4 servings.

Orange-Ginger Sauce

In medium saucepan combine ½ cup sugar, ¼ cup orange-flavored breakfast drink powder, 2 tablespoons cornstarch, 2 tablespoons finely snipped candied ginger, and dash salt. Stir in 1½ cups water. Cook and stir over medium-high heat till thickened and bubbly; cook 1 minute more. Remove from heat; stir in 2 tablespoons butter or margarine. Serve sauce warm over vanilla ice cream. Makes 1¾ cups.

Apple-Nut Dessert

Preheat oven to 350°. Combine 1 beaten egg, ½ cup sugar, and ½ teaspoon vanilla. Sift ½ cup all-purpose flour, 1 teaspoon baking powder, and ¼ teaspoon salt into egg mixture; mix well. Stir in 1 cup chopped tart apple and ¼ cup chopped walnuts. Spread in greased 10x6x2-inch baking pan. Bake at 350° till done, about 25 minutes. Cut into squares; serve warm topped with vanilla ice cream. Makes 6 servings.

Marshmallow Sauce

Into mixer bowl spoon one 7-, 9-, or 10-ounce jar marshmallow creme. Beating at high speed, gradually add ¼ cup pineapple juice. Continue beating till thick, 3 to 5 minutes. Fold in ¼ cup flaked coconut. Serve over sherbet. Makes 2 cups.

Apricot Mousse

1 2- or 2⅛-ounce package
  dessert topping mix
2 4½-ounce jars or cans strained
  apricots (baby food)
1 tablespoon honey

Prepare dessert topping mix according to package directions. Fold in apricots and honey. Spoon into dessert dishes; chill in freezer till served. Makes 6 servings.

Ruby Fruit Compote

Combine one 20-ounce can pitted tart red cherries, undrained, and 1¼ cups water. Blend 2 tablespoons *each* sugar and cornstarch and dash salt; stir into cherries. Add one 10-ounce package frozen red raspberries. Cook and stir till raspberries are thawed and mixture is bubbly. Add 1 pint fresh strawberries, washed, hulled, and halved; 1 tablespoon lemon juice; and 1 teaspoon vanilla. Cool slightly. Spoon into sherbet dishes; top with dollops of dairy sour cream. Serves 10 to 12.

Main Dish Preparation Times

INDEX